RADICAL RELIANCE

LIVING 24/7 *with* GOD *at the* CENTER

JOSEPH M. STOWELL

Discovery House Publishers

Books, music, and videos that feed the soul with the Word of God

Box 3566 Grand Rapids, MI 49501

Discovery House Publishers is affiliated with RBC Ministries,
Grand Rapids, Michigan.

Discovery House books are distributed to the trade exclusively by
Barbour Publishing, Inc., Uhrichsville, Ohio.

Requests for permission to quote from this book should be directed to:
Permissions Department, Discovery House Publishers,
P.O. Box 3566, Grand Rapids, MI 49501.

Unless otherwise indicated, Scripture quotations are from the
New American Standard Bible (NASB), ©1960, 1962, 1963, 1968, 1971,
1973, 1975, 1977, 1995 by The Lockman Foundation,
La Habra, California.

Paul Deutschman, "It Happened on the Brooklyn Subway."
Published in *Reader's Digest*, May 1949 by Paul Deutschman.
Reprinted by permission of Regina Ryan Publishing Enterprises, Inc.,
251 Central Park West, New York, New York 10024.

Library of Congress Cataloging-in-Publication Data
Stowell, Joseph M.
    [Far from home]
    Radical reliance : living 24/7 with God at the center / Joseph M.
      Stowell.
        p. m.
    Originally published: Far from home. Chicago: Moody Press, ©1998.
    Includes bibliographical references.
    ISBN 1-57293-188-4
  1. Spirituality. 2. Intimacy (Psychology) -- Religious aspects -- Christi-
    anity. I. Title.
    BV4501.3.S7695 2006
    248.4--dc22

                                                        2006008051

Interior design by Sherri L. Hoffman

Printed in the United States of America

08 09 10 11 12 / SB / 10 9 8 7 6 5 4

RADICAL RELIANCE

Other Books by Joseph M. Stowell

Eternity: Reclaiming a Passion for What Endures
From the Front Lines: Perspectives from the Trenches of Life
The Upside of Down: Finding Hope When It Hurts

========

God cannot give us a happiness and peace apart from Himself, because it is not there. There is no such thing.

—C. S. Lewis,
Mere Christianity

CONTENTS

ACKNOWLEDGMENTS

If you find the concepts of this book to be of help in satisfying the hunger in your soul for God, then thank . . .

Him for being so accessible;

The good folks at Discovery House, especially Carol Holquist and Judith Markham, for sharing in the vision for the importance of a book like this;

My wife, who gave up evenings and weekends so that I could finish the manuscript;

Beth Longjohn, my assistant, whose efficiency helps me clear out time to write;

None of us would be anything if it weren't for the gracious provision of the gifts and talents that God has given to equip and enable us to do His work. In that light, for whatever good that comes to you from the information in this book, give God the glory and enjoy the increasing pleasure of His company in your life.

INTRODUCTION: COMING HOME

The Pilgrimage Toward Intimacy

Several years ago, as I passed the fifty mark on the calendar of my life, I discovered a new and distinct desire to go deeper and pursue God more intentionally than ever before. I had dreamed a lot of dreams and seen many of them materialize. God, for reasons best known to Him, has been abundantly good to me. But after all those years of fast-paced busyness for Him and of conquering frontiers that loomed large in front of me, I found that beyond and under it all I still had a yearning in the core of my being that kept drawing my attention back to God.

While I have given God my best years and maximized my energies for Him, I have found that this busyness has not drawn me closer to Him. In fact, in some ways it creates a false and treacherous sense of spirituality. It leads to the assumption that spirituality is a performance and that intimacy with God is a business arrangement. Busyness creates a flat and dull sort of Christianity that can begin to turn our hearts cold and even sour if we are not careful.

I am awakening to the reality that we do ourselves no favors when we act and live as though Christianity were a stage on which we are to perform as though there were no deep need of an intimate relationship with the One who is the focus of our activity.

I have begun to sense as well that in the abundance of God's goodness to me I am prone to lose touch with the reality of how much I need Him. I know I need Him—my problem is that I find it easy to lose touch with the reality and ramifications of that knowledge. Early on in life and ministry my sense of need was apparent in that I earned less than our expenses, and without God's gracious, over-and-above financial provision, our family would not have made it. We needed Him. My insecurities as a minister and public figure kept me very much aware of how much I needed Him. Each new church that I shepherded challenged my sense of self-sufficiency. Becoming president of Moody Bible Institute only compounded my sense of need.

At the same time, God has given me gifts that enable me to be fruitful—just as He has for all believers. These gifts and His wisdom have made it possible for me to meet the challenges I have faced relatively well. I'm a third-generation minister, so some of my capacity for ministry is instinctive. My income, by His gracious provision, is now more than adequate. In time, I had served long enough at Moody to know the ropes and to enjoy what God had built me to do. And now, in my ministry of preaching and teaching God's Word, I find that after years of communicating His truths, it all comes quite naturally to me. All of these gifts of His grace threaten my *sense* of need for Him.

> *If I don't believe I need Him, I probably won't desire Him.*

But I do need Him. Desperately. Now more than ever.

In all of this soul-searching about longing for Him and needing Him, I have been and continue to be deeply committed to Him. I believe that I would die for Him if necessary. I have had the unexpected privilege of being used by Him in ways that I never dreamed or expected. Yet this longing in my soul is real, and I am realizing that my tendencies toward independence and self-sufficiency are debilitating my ability to get closer to Him. If I don't believe I need Him, I probably won't desire Him.

When we forget that we need Him, our Christianity becomes little more than a task maintained by responsibilities and requirements. He really doesn't need to do much for us. We are pretty well set. While we count on Him for the big things—redemption, bailing us out if life goes in the ditch (only to find that since we have failed to develop intimacy with Him in the good times we don't know how to reach for Him in the bad times)—we have missed the pleasure and wonder of needing Him and being in touch with His presence and power that alone can satisfy, sustain, and secure us as an ongoing experience of life.

The history of African-Americans in our country is one marked by the consciousness of needing God. As slaves they had little, life was hard, and there was no hope of gain or release. Yet their tradition is rich with a sense of reliance on God. It is evident in their music, as expressed in this spiritual:

Oh, when I am alone, when I am alone,
Oh, when I am alone, give me Jesus.
Give me Jesus, give me Jesus.
You may have all this world, give me Jesus.

God looks for this kind of adoring devotion and dependency from us, but for the most part He gets little of either.

How can we who have so much of the abundant gifts of His gracious bounty and who have the constant presence of God in and around our lives live at such a distance? How can we feel so alone at the depth of our own souls? Well, I've had enough. I've had enough of a life that keeps stalling on the way home. I live with a renewed desire for greater intimacy with God.

> *I want to go deeper with God. I am hearing the longing of my soul for more of Him.*

As stark as that sounds, that is really how I feel. And while my life has not been technically without God in some ways, it has been a life that has yet to cultivate the kind of adoring dependency that is required to experience Him most fully and to be most powerfully used of Him.

It's not that I haven't felt His touch. I have—in some very special ways. In fact, those periodic brushes with His wonderful reality are part of what drives me to live in the constancy of His touch. And it's not that I haven't loved Him. I do. It's that I stand ready and wanting to know more of Him and to know Him in a more personal and intimate way. I want to go deeper with God. I am hearing the longing of my soul for more of Him.

Want to come along?

This pilgrimage takes us to the center of our own being. Not that the pursuit of God is a selfish thing. It's that the center of our being is where God meets us. Following the allure of this longing takes us to our own souls. It is an intensely personal and ultimately an intimately pleasurable pursuit.

Realistically, we will never know intimacy with Him in the fullest measure. That is the privilege reserved for us when we step to the other side and have the lens of our souls wiped finally and fully clean to see Him face to face. But until then the healthiest and most fulfilling pursuit of life is to turn our lives toward that day and focus on getting as good a look as possible now—to connect with Him as intimately as permissible.

I'm struck by the fact that Scripture begins with Adam and Eve in a safe, satisfying fellowship with God. The rest of history is the story of humanity's attempt to live successfully apart from Him after being torn from Him by our self-sufficiency. Yet the search to find satisfaction within ourselves and the careful erection of structures that supposedly sustain us apart from God consistently fail. Not one has succeeded.

> *Life is best when it leans toward a deeper, more satisfying relationship with God.*

Only He can fill the void. He is what we are looking for. And in the end—which will be the eternal beginning—He will wipe away every tear and restore those who are His to that Eden-type of perfect fellowship forever, when we will triumphantly experience what John promises, "Behold, the tabernacle of God is among men, and He will dwell among them, and they shall be His people, and God Himself will be among them" (Revelation 21:3). And it is then that "happily ever after" will no longer be a dream or even a cynical laugh about the fairyland called eternal life. It will be a pulsating reality.

Until then, God beckons us to turn toward home—to begin the process of getting closer. To connect and enjoy Him and His resources more fully. He doesn't play cosmic games of hide-and-seek. He meets us where we are and helps us build momentum that drives us to Him. Life is best when it leans toward a deeper, more satisfying relationship with God. It is safest and most secure when we find our sustenance in all of life's situations in our connectedness to Him.

Regardless of who we are and what we have or do not have, the ultimate issue of life is *where do I look for real satisfaction, and where can I be assured of sufficient resources to sustain and secure me regardless?* If we don't seek to be satisfied and sustained in all the right places, we will finally be disappointed, left alone without hope and in despair.

Although these pages are among the first you will read of this book, they are the last I will write of it. As I lay down this manuscript, I must admit that I feel a sense of frustration, knowing that there is so much more I would like to say and certainly more that needs to be written about moving from a sense of soulish isolation to a satisfying experience of intimacy with God.

> *Like the Prodigal Son, we need to pick ourselves up and turn our hearts toward home.*

Therefore, until someone picks up this topic from here, let this book be a primer, a starting point in the wonderful adventure of finding satisfaction, security, and sustenance in a growing intimacy with God. In a sense this is a topic that will always beg for more, for we will never know intimacy in its fullest dimensions until we are truly home. But until then it is our privilege to begin the process of turning from the aloneness of our own self-sufficiency to the fullness of a connected, God-sufficient experience.

Intimacy and aloneness stand at the opposite ends of our existence. Throughout Scripture and the experience of humanity, aloneness is the judgment on a life that chooses to be satisfied and sustained apart from God. Like the Prodigal Son, we need to pick ourselves up and turn our hearts toward home. The Father is graciously waiting. When He sees us coming, He runs to meet us. He must wonder why it has taken so long.

one

FAR FROM HOME

Intimacy Reconsidered

DRAW NEAR TO GOD AND
HE WILL DRAW NEAR TO YOU.
—JAMES 4:8

Martha breathes a quiet sigh of relief as she realizes both the kids are napping. That doesn't happen often these days now that the older one is four. It seems that her entire life now revolves around the needs of two small children. Each day has become a continual cycle of feeding, cleaning up, doing laundry, telling stories, and playing on the floor. These precious moments for herself are few and far between.

She can't help but wonder what her life would be like if she hadn't had kids. Her husband drives off to the office each morning and seems oblivious to what he's leaving behind for her to do. When he comes home and complains about all the problems and injustices of his work, she can't help but feel a bit jealous. Five years ago she had a job of her own and was well on her way to becoming partner in a small but growing advertising agency. She would probably be making more than Fred by now, but she had devoted herself to motherhood. She loved her husband and kids, yet she couldn't help but miss the challenges of business and the interaction she had with fellow workers—opportunities to really use her mind. She feared she would never have that opportunity again.

But even then she knew that the money and stimulus of a challenging career would grow old and routine, leaving her looking for something that would really satisfy and sustain her soul.

Martha would tell you that what really haunts her is the memory of her former, uncluttered growing walk with Christ—before He was crowded out. Not intentionally. Just incrementally—bit by bit, choice by choice, busyness by busyness. Back then she was onto something deeper—something more satisfying.

Mark is in his early thirties. He is from a large, active family that was always involved in team sports and a variety of social activities. People his age don't play team sports so much any more, and golf isn't his idea of exercise. He and his wife of five years have prepared for a large family of their own but are having trouble getting pregnant. An emptiness nags him. No longer does he have the bustle of activity around him all the time. His house seems eerie and quiet, which makes him uncomfortable. He and his wife have talked so much about their situation that neither of them has much to say anymore.

Church and his experience of Christianity have become routine and flat. He and his wife stay in the routines and rituals of their commitment to Christ, but any sense of meaning and fulfillment is sporadic at best. Their lives for the most part are no different from the lives of those millions who have no connection to Christ.

He is beginning to lose hope that his life will ever be anything close to what he had planned. His wife, too, seems to be suffering from an inner depression she can hardly admit to herself, much less to him. But how can he help her when he doesn't know how to handle the submerged vacancy in his own soul?

THE SEARCH FOR SATISFACTION

I'm not much for jigsaw puzzles, but I know enough about them to know that you need all the pieces to enjoy a satisfying outcome. In many ways life is like a thousand-piece puzzle. We spend our days putting it together, hoping to create something meaningful out of all the scattered pieces. But when we can't find the strategic pieces that complete the picture, we face unsettling disappointment at best, and, at worst, despair.

Honest philosophers have been telling us for centuries that life left to itself can be lonely, meaningless, and empty. Disappointment and despair are to be expected as normal by-products of our existence. The remedies proposed range from the passive resignation of a life stuck in the byword *whatever* to engagement in any experience that provides the adrenaline rush of temporary hits of excitement. Even the writer of Ecclesiastes searched the depths of wisdom, pleasure, wealth, and work to find meaning and satisfaction but came up disillusioned. His conclusion is painstakingly honest.

> *Then I became great and increased more than all who preceded me in Jerusalem. My wisdom also stood by me. All that my eyes desired I did not refuse them. I did not withhold my heart from any pleasure, for my heart was pleased because of all my labor and this was my reward for all my labor. Thus I considered all my activities which my hands had done and the labor which I had exerted, and behold all was vanity and striving after wind and there was no profit under the sun (Ecclesiastes 2:9–11).*

As one observer notes, "Life is like a wild goose chase without the goose."

In our most honest moments, we have all wondered why life is not more rewarding. Even our best experiences rarely leave much of lasting value, and often the anticipation is more fulfilling than the experience itself. We "channel surf" life, looking—hoping—for something to catch our attention, only to end up bored, jaded, and flat. And when life gets in our face, we are shocked at how brutal and unconsoling it can be. In our quiet moments we feel stalked by a sense of emptiness and fear.

When God is banished from human experience or relegated to the religious margins of our lives, left only to serve us on an "on-call" basis, we become functionally alone.

We wonder, "Why? . . . What is missing?"

Has anyone noticed that the one thing the philosophers, the meaning-searcher in Ecclesiastes, and many of us have in common is that God has been removed as the preeminent center of our existence? When God is banished from human experience or relegated to the religious margins of our lives, left only to serve us on an "on-call" basis, we become functionally alone. And in that aloneness, emptiness and vulnerability become more than philosophical theory. They are naked reality.

Are followers of Christ exempt?

No.

Even those of us who are connected to God through redemption often live our lives as though He isn't particularly relevant to the everyday occasions and encounters of life. We are proficient at maintaining the level of religious activity we deem appropriate, but God is hardly the throbbing center of our lives.

Yet He is supposed to be. And until He is, life is always less—far less—than it could be. Sometimes tragically less.

Unfortunately, we get used to life at a distance from God and become resigned to its not being what it is cracked up to be. We end up thinking that a close, satisfying relationship with God is only what others experience. And even though He has offered us nearness, God seems inaccessibly far away.

And so we give up. Like paraplegic war veterans, we know how much we miss what we've lost, but, having no hope of getting it back, we adjust.

But life at a distance always has its downside. Not being in touch with God makes it difficult to depend and rely on Him. Living at a distance makes it easier to sin and to live in our sin—which only extends the distance. A creeping, quiet cynicism numbs our souls. When we hear the refrain, "Draw near to God and He will draw near to you" (James 4:8), we relegate it to the category of biblical statements we must believe but will probably never experience.

Yet the statement is true!

Those who draw near to God *do* find Him drawing near to them. God is the rewarder of those who "diligently seek him" (Hebrews 11:6 KJV). There are legions that could testify to the pleasure of the experience.

The fault is not God's. We are not victims of some cosmic scam.

A PRODIGAL'S STORY

Who bears the responsibility for our distance from God becomes clear in the parable of the prodigal son, found in Luke 15:11–32, perhaps Jesus' best-known and most-retold story. It is reflective of our experience with God, for in some measure the Prodigal's story is ours too.

The parable begins: "A man had two sons. The younger of them said to his father, 'Father, give me the share of the estate that falls to me.' So he divided his wealth between them" (Luke 15:11-12).

We aren't told why the younger son made this request. It wasn't even protocol for him to do so. Perhaps he felt like the low man on the totem pole in his household. Maybe he had a passion to make a name for himself. Maybe the older brother was hassling him. Maybe he was just bored. But it is safe to speculate that in addition to any other reasons he may have had for leaving, chief among them was that he didn't know what a good thing he had. He lived in comfort and safety with a loving father, but this seemed tame compared with the allure of the world outside.

So he chose to leave.

And his father, for whatever reason, granted the request. He gave his son his portion of the inheritance and the freedom to walk away—and watched as he took to the road, intent on reaching a far country where he could live a more exciting life.

God is like that father, and often we are prone to be like that son. When we say that God is far away, it is we who have left, not He. Perhaps we have consciously or unconsciously held God at arms' length. We have wanted Him, but not wanted Him to interfere. Or we have feared that He would demand too much and that, having Him, we would have nothing else. Or our lives are so full of His abundant bounty that we have come to believe that we are not truly alone without Him—that we have all we need; that we really don't need Him. Or we may not have known how to draw near. Or the pace and crush of life has kept us from pursuing what we *do* know about intimacy with God.

Whatever the reason, our lives are the poorer for it. In fact, our lives are at risk because of it. The farther we are from God, the farther we are from the three essential ingredients we really need—really want—out of life. It is He who wants, and He alone who is able to *satisfy, sustain*, and *secure* us. Without Him we are too frail to ward off the forces of life that are beyond our control. We are too compulsive, shortsighted, and misguided to find in-depth satisfaction and sustenance on our own. And when He is at a distance, we are easy targets for Satan's seductive allures. Sin and its debilitating consequences lie in ambush for those who stray far from God.

We are the prodigals. It is we who have left home. We are the ones who have been seduced and consumed by lesser allures. We, not God, are in the far country, and when we come to know how wonderful He is and how alone and empty we are, our hearts will long for home.

Tracking toward intimacy with God is not a nice thing to do. It is a necessary pursuit if we are to be safe in life and fulfilled at the core of our being. To experience life as He meant it to be, to be fulfilled as He intends us to be, and sustained and secure as He wishes us to be means that we begin the rewarding adventure of closing the gap.

> *It is He who wants, and He alone who is able to* satisfy, *sustain, and* secure *us.*

Wanting Him and Him alone to fill our empty hearts, we pick up what is left of ourselves and head for home. At first we find it difficult to see clearly down the road, but with the help of other pilgrims we soon catch our pace, and the nearer we draw the more familiar the landmarks become. There's the church that we attend, and as we pass we see the days gone by when our hearts filled with joy as we sang His praises and served His people. There's the park bench where we used to sit and feel His closeness as we contemplated the beauty and wonder of His creation. And our Bible. And that special room where we spent precious times of fellowship with God in prayer. And our friends, who used to hold us accountable. We can still remember those times of prayer on Saturday mornings with them.

Who is that running to meet us?

Could it be God? We've been away so long, and our choice to live in the far country has been such a sadness, such an offense to Him.

What we have not known is that His face has been turned toward the horizon watching, waiting to see if today might be the day we would come home. He's been there all the time.

It is He. His compassion embraces us. We are stunned by His grace and fall in humble repentance at His feet. He lifts us up and turns us toward home. He calls for the robe, the ring, and the sandals. He begins the celebration and demands the fatted calf.

For the first time in a long time we feel how good it is to be home where we belong. Chasing the aloneness into the shadows begins by seeking our satisfaction and sustenance at home—where God is.

While we have life and breath, God will not cease to pursue a rewarding, deepening intimacy with us. He is not content to leave us alone. His unceasing, unconditional love for each of us compels Him. He wants to meet us at the intersection of every dream, every desire, every choice, and every thought, and He urges us to turn toward Him and actualize the finished work of His Son, the gift of the Spirit, and the resource of His Word. He welcomes us to begin a pilgrimage that puts our backs toward the aloneness in our souls and turns our faces toward the spectacular glow of intimacy with Him—toward life the way it was meant to be.

> *While we have life and breath, God will not cease to pursue a rewarding, deepening intimacy with us.*

REUNION

In the book *Great Stories Remembered*, Paul Deutschman tells the story of an incredible reunion. The almost unbelievable dynamics of this story are a metaphor for the unexpected and urgent potential that we too can be reunited with our God and fulfill our hopes for the intimacy that once lived within our hearts when we were wed to Him at the cross.

Marcel Sternberger was a methodical man of nearly 50, with bushy white hair, guileless brown eyes, and the bouncing enthusiasm of a czardas dancer of his native Hungry. He always took the 9:09 Long Island

Railroad train from his suburban home to Woodside, N.Y., where he caught a subway into the city.

On the morning of January 10, 1948, Sternberger boarded the 9:09 as usual. En route, he suddenly decided to visit Laszlo Victor, a Hungarian friend who lived in Brooklyn and was ill.

Accordingly, at Ozone Park, Sternberger changed to the subway for Brooklyn, went to his friend's house, and stayed until midafternoon. He then boarded a Manhattan-bound subway for his Fifth Avenue office. Here is Marcel's incredible story:

> The car was crowded, and there seemed to be no chance of a seat. But just as I entered, a man sitting by the door suddenly jumped up to leave, and I slipped into the empty place.
>
> I've been living in New York long enough not to start conversations with strangers. But, being a photographer, I have the peculiar habit of analyzing people's faces, and I was struck by the feature of the passenger on my left. He was probably in his late 30's, and when he glanced up, his eyes seemed to have a hurt expression in them. He was reading a Hungarian-language newspaper, and something prompted me to say in Hungarian, "I hope you don't mind if I glance at your paper."
>
> The man seemed surprised to be addressed in his native language. But he answered politely. "You may read it now. I'll have time later on."
>
> During the half-hour ride to town, we had quite a conversation. He said his name was Bela Paskin. A law student when World War II started, he had been put into a German labor battalion and sent to the Ukraine. Later he was captured by the Russians and put to work burying the German dead. After the war, he covered hundreds of miles on foot until he reached his home in Debrecen, a large city in eastern Hungary.
>
> I myself knew Debrecen quite well, and we talked about it for a while. Then he told me the rest of his story. When he went to the apartment once occupied by his father, mother, brothers and sisters, he found strangers living there. Then he went upstairs to

the apartment that he and his wife once had. It also was occupied by strangers. None of them had ever heard of his family.

As he was leaving, full of sadness, a boy ran after him, calling "Paskin bacsi! Paskin bacsi!" That means "Uncle Paskin." The child was the son of some old neighbors of his. He went to the boy's home and talked to his parents. "Your whole family is dead," they told him. "The Nazis took them and your wife to Auschwitz."

Auschwitz was one of the worst Nazi concentration camps. Paskin gave up all hope. A few days later, too heartsick to remain any longer in Hungary, he set out again on foot, stealing across border after border until he reached Paris. He managed to immigrate to the United States in October 1947, just three months before I met him.

All the time he had been talking, I kept thinking that somehow his story seemed familiar. A young woman whom I had met recently at the home of friends had also been from Debrecen; she had been sent to Auschwitz; from there she had been transferred to work in a German munitions factory. Her relatives had been killed in the gas chambers. Later, she was liberated by the Americans and was brought here in the first boatload of displaced persons in 1946.

Her story had moved me so much that I had written down her address and phone number, intending to invite her to meet my family and thus help relieve the terrible emptiness in her life.

It seemed impossible that there could be any connection between these two people, but as I neared my station, I fumbled anxiously in my address book. I asked in what I hoped was a casual voice, "Was your wife's name Marya?"

He turned pale. "Yes!" He answered. "How did you know?" He looked as if he were about to faint.

I said, "Let's get off the train." I took him by the arm at the next station and led him to a phone booth. He stood there like a man in a trance while I dialed her phone number.

It seemed hours before Marya Paskin answered. (Later I learned her room was alongside the telephone, but she was in the habit of never answering it because she had so few friends and the calls were always for someone else. This time, however, there was no one else at home and, after letting it ring for a while, she responded.)

When I heard her voice at last, I told her who I was and asked her to describe her husband. She seemed surprised at the question, but gave me a description. Then I asked her where she had lived in Debrecen, and she told me the address.

Asking her to hold the line, I turned to Paskin and said, "Did you and your wife live on such-and-such a street?"

"Yes!" Bela exclaimed. He was white as a sheet and trembling.

"Try to be calm," I urged him. "Something miraculous is about to happen to you. Here, take this telephone and talk to your wife!"

He nodded his head in mute bewilderment, his eyes bright with tears. He took the receiver, listened a moment to his wife's voice, then suddenly cried, "This is Bela! This is Bela!" and he began to mumble hysterically. Seeing that the poor fellow was so excited he couldn't talk coherently, I took the receiver from his shaking hands.

"Stay where you are," I told Marya, who also sounded hysterical. "I am sending your husband to you. We will be there in a few minutes."

Bela was crying like a baby and saying over and over again, "It is my wife. I go to my wife!"

At first I thought I had better accompany Paskin, lest the man should faint from excitement, but I decided that this was a moment in which no strangers should intrude. Putting Paskin into a taxicab, I directed the driver to take him to Marya's address, paid the fare, and said goodbye.

Bela Paskin's reunion with his wife was a moment so poignant, so electric with suddenly released emotion, that afterward neither he nor Marya could recall much about it.

"I remember only that when I left the phone, I walked to the mirror like in a dream to see if maybe my hair had turned gray," she said later. "The next thing I know, a taxi stops in front of the house, and it is my husband who comes toward me. Details I cannot remember; only this I know—that I was happy for the first time in many years . . .

"Even now it is difficult to believe that it happened. We have both suffered so much; I have almost lost the capability to not be afraid. Each time my husband goes from the house I say to myself, 'Will anything happen to take him from me again?' "

Her husband is confident that no horrible misfortune will ever again befall them. "Providence has brought us together," he says simply. "It was meant to be."

Skeptical persons will no doubt attribute the events of that memorable afternoon to mere chance. But was it chance that made Marcel Sternberger suddenly decide to visit his sick friend and hence take a subway line that he had never ridden before? Was it chance that caused the man sitting by the door of the car to rush out just as Sternberger came in? Was it chance that caused Bela Paskin to be sitting beside Sternberger, reading a Hungarian newspaper?

> *God waits patiently, yet insistently, for us to let Him give us His unhindered satisfaction, sustenance, and security.*

Was it chance—or did God ride the Brooklyn subway that afternoon?

As significant and as urgent as this life-changing reunion became to Bela Paskin, our reunion to a nearer, deepening relationship with our God is of great urgency and offers a far more wonderful reward. We would weep with regret if we knew what we are missing in a life that knows about Him but rarely if ever feels His touch. His Spirit keeps urging us to live on a better plane while we seem content to ride this subway of our lives in the routine normalcy of a self-imposed emptiness. We need not live alone. God waits patiently, yet insistently, for us to let Him give us His unhindered satisfaction, sustenance, and security.

Welcome to an adventure that pursues an adoring dependence on the One who will not leave us alone—the One who will never leave us and never forsake us. Denying ourselves the privilege of the intimacy that was so extravagantly purchased for us at the cross is to leave ourselves struggling with the aloneness that the distance inflicts on our souls.

two

ALONENESS

The Jeopardy of Life Apart from God

Thou hast made us for Thyself and our hearts are
restless until they find their all in Thee.
—Augustine

Nigel and Margaret run a bed-and-breakfast in the remote country-side of England. It's so remote that my wife and I got lost twice trying to locate it. I'd still be driving around if Martie hadn't suggested that we stop to ask for directions. When we finally arrived, Nigel met us outside. The aristocratic twist to his English accent raised the suspicion that most likely he hadn't lived in the country all his life. As we went in we met Margaret, who welcomed us warmly. Going down the hall to our room, I couldn't help but notice the beautiful pieces of art and the pictures of Nigel and Margaret with people who clearly were significant.

My inquisitive mind was engaged. *Why are people who are obviously from a privileged class spending their retirement years running a B&B?*

We were their only guests, and they invited us to join them and a friend for dinner. In the course of the conversation, I asked what they had done before they retired. I was hoping to get a clue to satisfy my nagging curiosity. Nigel obligingly told me the whole story.

They had moved to Hong Kong forty-three years before to work for the British government. After a few years Nigel began a business distributing skiwear to posh resorts in Australia, America, and Britain. The business mushroomed, and for years he and Margaret belonged to the best clubs, moved in high society, and traveled to exotic resorts around the world. Then, just before their retirement, the recessions then sweeping through America and England cut the legs out from under his business. One creditor went into bankruptcy, owing Nigel's company nine million dollars. Others did the same, unable to pay him what he was owed. He was forced to close his business, having lost almost everything. He and Margaret packed their remaining belongings and got on a freighter. They arrived in England twenty-seven days later.

All that had satisfied, sustained, and secured them had evaporated.

Nigel and Margaret were threatened by life's most debilitating reality. *Aloneness.* The kind of aloneness that threatens all of us. The aloneness that arrives full force when all the props we depended on are kicked out from under us and we are left naked in the face of the overwhelming realities of life.

But it's not always loss that magnifies our emptiness and gives us a haunting sense of aloneness. An Ohio man won $7.5 million. He had been earning $14,000 a year, which jumped immediately to nearly $300,000 a year. He built himself a $170,000 house but didn't find the satisfaction he had expected. In fact, he was quoted as saying his life had become a "living hell" because people were demanding money from him. A few years after he won the jackpot, he set fire to his house. When the police came and arrested him for aggravated arson, he asked if they could move the police car he was in so he could get a better view of the blaze.

> *Aloneness is what we feel when we are functionally disconnected at the core of our being from all that truly satisfies, sustains, and secures.*

This man beat the odds to win something he thought would bring contentment to his life. But it didn't work out that way. Whatever he plugged into the equation came up short, and he was left alone.

ALONENESS

Aloneness is what we feel when we are *functionally disconnected at the core of our being from all that truly satisfies, sustains, and secures.* It is the absence of an experiential sense of God's presence, power, and pleasure to supply us with the resources that support all of life. It is the ultimate consequence of trusting in comparisons and commodities that are, at the end of the day, insufficient.

And just in case we mistakenly assume that this is a problem exclusively for those who do not belong to God, look at the lives of many of us who call ourselves by His name. It is easy to see that we are often far less than satisfied with our lives. In crisis we are equally unprepared to be sustained. We are just as prone to assume that the real source of satisfaction and sustenance is in the pleasure and properties that the world provides. When life goes south on us, we can sometimes be as negative, cynical, pessimistic, and despairing as the guy next door.

There are many of us who are outwardly exemplary Christians whose lives reflect that we really don't rely on God but rather on others and ourselves. It's why we struggle with covetousness and jealous feelings toward others who have a better lot in life or more than we have materially. If God were our sufficient source of satisfaction and sustenance, we would reflect contentment with Him and be able to rejoice with others who are more blessed with material goods or a smoother life. If we lived connectedly we would not become bitter when life disappoints us because we wouldn't be looking to life as our source of satisfaction in the first place. We would, in fact, be more grateful when God chose to bless us with good things. We would not react and respond to life's situations intuitively but would connect to His wisdom and ways and be satisfied to be counted faithful even in the midst of loss and suffering. We could suffer the loss of money, friends, family, and even health and be unshaken, for though we loved and enjoyed the privilege of all we possess, we never counted on those things to ultimately satisfy.

If we do not live in a primary connectedness with God as our ultimate source, aloneness will deal us a devastating hand when our parents break up. When our spouse packs up and leaves. When our career goals are thwarted. When our children turn their backs on us and abandon the values we feel are significant. When large and strategic dreams of life explode in our face. It will be the author of ongoing agony when marriage, friends, or careers turn out to be less fulfilling than we had imagined. When health suddenly fails. When prosperity fails to fulfill us. When we get old and there is little of value left in our lives. It's the haunting emptiness we feel when we look back on a life that was busy and even prosperous, yet of little or no significance.

Aloneness is the gnawing despair of being rejected by those we love the most. It's how we feel when we are emotionally marginalized and put off to the side in groups or networks we value. Aloneness is the deepening frustration of not having the answers to troubling situations or the solutions to insurmountable problems. It's how we feel when we fail and no one understands or cares or when we suffer great loss and all those around us get on with their lives as though nothing had happened.

It is the consequence of a life that has failed to cultivate a deepening relationship with the resources that satisfy, sustain, and secure us regardless of what happens.

Aloneness marks our lives with cynicism. It carves a hollowness within us that alters our tone and perspective on life. When we realize that we are truly alone at the core of our being, life becomes routine and flat, something to get through. Something to fill with immediate hits of gratification to drown out the meaninglessness and purposelessness that we feel. In its advanced stages, aloneness brands our deepest selves with despair and hopelessness. It covers life with a cloud of cynical pessimism that produces a "Who cares?" . . . "Whatever!" response. It's a deadening and darkening blow to the life and light in our souls. It's life without wind in our sails.

I'm not an old salt, but I've sailed enough to know that there are two problems you don't want to have: being becalmed or being overblown. *Becalmed* means there's not enough wind to propel the craft; *overblown* is having more wind than your sails can cope with, causing you to pull in your sails and ride out the gale at the mercy of the storm.

Aloneness is life without the thrill and wonder of God in our sails. When tragedy hits it's not having sufficient sail to produce confidence and security in the midst of the storm. This functional disconnectedness from sustaining resources leaves us living somewhere between a life that is boring and a life that is beyond our ability to cope. Some of us are scurrying about somewhere in between the ends of the continuum. Eventually we will be at one end or the other.

BEYOND LONELINESS

Aloneness is different from sought-after times of being by ourselves, and it is far more significant than being lonely. Being physically alone is often a coveted experience. It is therapy from the busyness and fast-paced confusion of life. It helps us to get in touch with ourselves, our values, and our priorities. Every mother knows the treasure of hours—or minutes—when at last she is alone.

Christ often went apart to find spiritual renewal, solace in times of grief, and rest from the crush and demanding pace of a people-intensive ministry. One of the most touching moments of Christ's humanity was when He withdrew to a place of solitude after He heard of the beheading of John the Baptist. John was Christ's cousin. But more significantly, he had been martyred for announcing the coming of Christ. Matthew tells us that Jesus, when He heard of this savage and cruel tragedy, struck by a sense of personal loss, "withdrew from there in a boat to a secluded place by Himself" (Matthew 14:13). Interrupted in His solitude by people who followed Him, He took His boat ashore and ministered, healing and feeding the five thousand. The text then says that He told His disciples to go to the other side of the sea and sent the multitudes away and "went up on the mountain by Himself to pray; and when it was evening, He was there alone" (v. 23). It was in these times of being alone that He dealt with His grief and refreshed His reserves to live and serve for another season effectively.

I am an incurable, unrepentant people person. Yet after a busy day full of people encounters, getting in the car to drive home can be an ecstatic experience. I'm all by myself, with only me to manage and the freedom to listen to whatever I want to on the radio. But when people are by themselves for extended times of isolation, then a sense of loneliness begins to ooze in on the edges of life.

When loneliness comes, it is often complicated by feelings of rejection, insecurity, self-doubt, and self-pity. Yet being lonely is only the surface blush of aloneness. Generally, being lonely means that we are without people and are denied experiential relationships with significant others. Loneliness is what the marooned man experienced when a genie on the deserted island gave him and his friends just one wish. One said that he wished to go home to his brokerage firm in Boston, while the other wished to go home to Chicago to be with his family. In a flash they were gone. The remaining one of the three looked around and said, "It's so lonely here, I wish my friends were back."

Loneliness is *external*. The cure for loneliness is a changed environment. Cultivating friendships or restoring past or broken relationships can repair it.

> *Aloneness is internal.*
> *It is a condition of the*
> *soul, heart, and mind.*

Aloneness is *internal*. It is a condition of the soul, heart, and mind. You can be in a crowd of intimate friends who fill you with companionship and still be alone in your soul. The popular Eastern mystic and philosopher, J. Krishnamurti, speaking the aloneness so prevalent in our culture (but using the term *loneliness*), rightly concludes:

> You may lose yourself in a crowd, and yet be utterly lonely; you may be intensely active, but loneliness creeps up on you; put the book down, and it is there. Amusements and drinks cannot drown out loneliness; you may temporarily evade it, but when the laughter and the effects of alcohol are over, the fear of loneliness returns.

He continues:

> You may be ambitious and successful, you may have vast powers over others, you may be rich in knowledge, you may worship and forget yourself in a rigmarole of rituals; but do what you will, the ache of loneliness continues . . . You may love or hate, escape from it according to your temperament and psychological demands; but loneliness is there, waiting and watching, withdrawing only to approach again.[1]

GOD'S COMPANIONSHIP

It is into the certainty of this soulish sense of aloneness that Scripture makes a bold and unqualified claim. I hope you will listen carefully as though you were being told the most important piece of advice that you have heard or will ever hear. You must resist the temptation to gloss this reality with pious thoughts and spiritualized irrelevancies. When you have heard this claim, stop reading. Put this book on your lap, descend into the depths of your soul, and consider the life-transforming breadth and depth of this truth.

The truth is this: *Only* God is capable of providing the companionship that chases our aloneness into the shadows. Only He can satisfy, sustain, and secure us.

Don't read any further until you have attempted to wrap your mind and heart around this truth and its ramifications. Its implications are radical and its application life-changing—even life-threatening.

> *The truth is this: Only God is capable of providing the companionship that chases our aloneness into the shadows.*

As Nigel was finishing his story of all that they had lost, Margaret interrupted and said, "But don't feel sorry for us Through it all we had our God and each other. We could have never made it without the sustaining reality of our relationship with God and the support that we found as we prayed together. In fact, we are actually happier now than we were then with all our money and status."

Granted, God often satisfies, secures, and sustains through His gift of trusted relationships and provisions from the material order, but ultimately, as Nigel and Margaret experienced, when all else fails *it is He and He alone who is our sufficient companion.*

Maybe we know this but have been afraid to put all our eggs in the basket of His generously offered resources. Perhaps our fear is reflected in the words of the poet who wrote, "lest having Him I would have nothing else beside." Losing control of the careful crafting and management of our own satisfaction and security is a threatening thought. So we are prone to connect with the secondary sources and take the primary source for granted, leaving us weak and vulnerable when the secondary sources fail. Placing our bets on anything else but God leaves us ultimately alone in good times as well as bad.

And as much as we are prone to live in denial about our soulish distance from God, in actuality we do tend to cultivate our confidence in all the lesser things. Our lack of connectedness to God as the singular source for everything in life proves the point. When was the last time we worshiped God by telling Him that all we need and all that is important to us in life is *Him*? And that if all were to be stripped from us we would still be fulfilled in the richness of the satisfaction we have found in our relationship with Him. That if earthly props were gone we would be *confident* in the sustaining reality of His character and provisions that we have already learned to trust in and enjoy. That if we become threatened by forces above and beyond ourselves we would respond with fearless *courage* since we have cultivated a relationship with Him that has learned the peace of responding with the psalmist who said,

> The LORD is my light and my salvation;
> Whom shall I fear?
> The LORD is the defense of my life;
> Whom shall I dread? . . .
> Though a host encamp against me,
> My heart will not fear;
> Though war arise against me,
> In spite of this I shall be confident (Psalm 27:1, 3).

It would be revealing if we were to honestly list the sources of satisfaction and sustenance in our lives. My guess is that those of us who have been blessed with a relatively sane and prosperous life would put things like home, family, friends, a great day at the mall, income, passions, work, vacations, a cottage by the lake, and a good game of golf on a perfect summer day near the top.

For many of us, God might not even make the list until someone reminded us that He should be there. And if He did, He would no doubt be one item among many others. If someone were to ask how He satisfies and sustains in the daily experience of life, I wonder what our response would be.

A life that lacks intimacy with God is a life that is truly alone. *Intimacy is what we experience as we grow more deeply conscious of, connected to, and confident in Him and Him alone as our unfailing resource in life.* But when we are self-satisfied and self-sustained under the veneer of a rote and ritualistic relationship to Him, we have set up residence in the far country.

> *Intimacy is what we experience as we grow more deeply conscious of, connected to, and confident in Him and Him alone as our unfailing resource in life*

In the far country there is no lack of everything we think we want or need. There is even room for religious activity and pious endeavors. But there is also an echo of emptiness, a groaning beneath the surface that is always there. Something is missing—and that something is God. He doesn't live there. He is at home, where we belong. The wonderful reality is that the truly good things we enjoy in the far country are in His home as well. The difference is that He is there. In His home His gifts to us are for our enjoyment. They are not seen as sources that ultimately satisfy and secure. As Paul says, it is "God . . . who richly supplies us with all things to enjoy" (1 Timothy 6:17). When we are at home with Him, we don't bank on the lesser stuff to satisfy our souls. We are connected to Him and tap Him as the source.

NEVER ALONE

When we become increasingly connected with God, we can experience *loneliness* but not be *alone* in terms of what is truly sustaining in life. Christ was often lonely. He was rejected, marginalized, misunderstood, and never fully appreciated for who He was. He had a deep sense of being ostracized; yet in the midst of this loneliness He was never alone. John 8:29 records Christ's confidence when He says, "He who sent Me is with Me; He has not left Me alone." And even though He realized His teaching was rejected by men, He concluded, "My judgment is true; for I am not *alone* in it, but I and the Father who sent Me" (John 8:16, italics added). On one occasion He spoke of the difference between being left alone and aloneness when he said, "An hour is coming . . . for you to be scattered, each to his own home, and to leave Me alone; and yet I am not alone, because the Father is with Me" (John 16:32).

The strength of Christ's life and ministry lay in His prioritized connectedness to His Father as His ultimate resource for satisfaction, sustenance, and security. In fact, the deepest agony of the cross was when Christ cried out, "My God, my God, why hast thou forsaken me?" (Matthew 27:46 KJV). That was the cry of aloneness.

Loneliness is *temporary*. When a person does not connect to God as the source, aloneness is *inevitable*. I am convinced that the ultimate terror of hell will not be Satan, the demons, the fire, or the terrible environment but rather the realization that for eternity there will be no hope of God. And there will be no external companionships or commodities to cover our deep need to know intimacy with God. Aloneness—forever—in its rarest, most desperate form is the agony of hell.

It's not that the things and thrills of this world don't temporarily satisfy and sustain. It's that at best they are like fireworks on the shoreline of life, lighting the night of our lives with transitory rushes of excitement. But then the night is there again.

And we are alone.

Really alone.

A PRODIGAL'S PROGRESS

When the Prodigal Son walked away from home, his heart was full of adventure and his pockets full of cash. No doubt he was thrilled to be on his own. *Peace and quiet at last. My own boss.* The potential problem of aloneness was the farthest thing from his mind.

We too feel pressured, busy, and crowded, and we crave solitude. Yet simply being by ourselves won't guarantee the peace we want. We may enjoy the quiet for a while, but the feeling is deceptive. If we don't have that inner sense of fulfillment only God can provide, we won't be any happier by ourselves than we were when we were one of the crowd.

At what point does solitude become loneliness? At what point does loneliness degenerate into aloneness? I think the timetables are different depending on our personalities, but without the practice of God's presence in our lives and the intimacy that only He provides, the process always is a downward spiral into aloneness.

The Prodigal Son didn't get far from home overnight. Don't you suppose he felt a twinge of homesickness his first night on the road? Surely he was beginning to realize that what he was gaining in individual freedom he was sacrificing in relational intimacy. If he had turned around at that point, he wouldn't have suffered much. But he kept on. In the wrong direction. Farther and farther from home.

three

INTIMACY IN PERSPECTIVE

The Trouble with What We Have

HE WHO HAS NO NEED BECAUSE HE IS SUFFICIENT FOR HIMSELF,
MUST EITHER BE A BEAST OR A GOD.
—ARISTOTLE

Bob and Ginger had not been married long before they realized that they were blazing career trails that would be very rewarding. They built their dream home, joined the right clubs, and over the years accumulated more money than they needed. They had three smartly dressed children, were able to afford a live-in babysitter, and sent their children to the best private schools.

Both Bob and Ginger had been reared in godly homes and, in the midst of their affluence, remained involved in their church. They attended when they were in town and did their best to encourage the pastor and participate in the church's ministries. But like many other Christians, their personal walk with Christ was more a matter of ritualistic responsibility than the passionate pursuit of their lives. For them, the real sources of satisfaction, security, and sustenance lay in the seemingly impenetrable fortresses of wealth, social networks, and treasures they had amassed.

Interestingly, even though their lives were focused on social status and material well being, many in the church Bob and Ginger attended looked to them as role models. While most of the church family were average and even lower than average in terms of material blessings, they too had lives that appeared to be committed to Christ yet remained distant from an intimate connection with Him. In fact most of them wished they could be like Bob and Ginger. *That would be life at its best,* they thought. The idea that satisfaction, security, and sustenance come from what we can gain from the companions and commodities around us was a life-defining assumption for them.

When our spirituality is characterized by self-sufficiency rather than God-sufficiency, we rarely feel the need to depend on God, and our souls are not consumed with a passionate desire for Him. Instead we are prone to long for God only in times of impending need or when earthly things have proven to be unrewarding. We long for Him in the tough times instead of cultivating a daily, ongoing, deepening relationship to Him as the only genuine source of true satisfaction. He is there in case we *might* need Him, not because we think we do need Him. He functions as the divine "911" of our lives. When life cruises on a level plane, though we might never admit it, we have the sense that we don't need God. Not *really*.

But the psalmist reflects a dramatically and refreshingly different perspective. His yearnings set Him apart from most of us. God is the focus of his *dependence* and his *desire*. He likens himself to the deer that depends on water to survive and therefore deeply desires what he so acutely needs.

As the deer pants for the water brooks,
So my soul pants for You, O God.
My soul thirsts for God, for the living God;
When shall I come and appear before God? (Psalm 42:1-2).

Once when we were traveling in the Middle East, Martie and I booked a ride on a camel safari in the desert of the United Arab Emirates. We rocked on top of those ugly beasts for an hour as we perused the quiet desolation of the desert. In the course of describing the attributes of camels, our guide mentioned that camels can go for three months without drinking. Those guys are obviously built for the desert.

What a contrast these plodding animals—that look like a horse put together by a committee—are to the sleek, type-A gazelle the psalmist had in mind when He revealed that his soul's desire for God was like the thirst the deer feels as he pants for the water brooks. Bounding through the meadows and the forests, the deer is satisfied and sustained on a regular basis with water. He needs it and yearns for it in his fast-paced existence.

After our intriguing desert experience, it crossed my mind that many of us are more like the camel than the deer. Rarely sensing our need for God, we go for months without desiring Him. In fact, for some of us, life has been a long stretch of religious activity without any sense of dependence on or desire for God. The problem is that we weren't built for a life in a spiritual desert. We were built for regular satisfying access to the refreshing presence of God in our souls.

> *We were built for regular satisfying access to the refreshing presence of God in our souls.*

Why would the composer of Psalm 42 express such an acute longing for God? At first blush, we might think he is in deep trouble or has a deep desire he wants God to fulfill. Yet surprisingly there does not appear to be a pressing material crisis or special reason for him to appeal for largess. Adequately supplied with health and wealth, the psalmist's pressing need is simply to experience the presence and the pleasure of God in the depths of his being, and that conviction drives His desire for intimacy with God.

We find the psalmist where the Jews have often found themselves in their history: in exile. As an exile, he is removed from the presence of God in Jerusalem. He wistfully remembers the days of worshiping God in the temple and experiencing His pleasure during the great festivals of Israel. Thus removed from God, he feels the loss and longs to experience God again as the source of his satisfaction.

The text goes on to say that the pagans chide him for not looking to their gods of wood and stone and mock his tenacious allegiance to the God of his soul. They taunt, "Where is your God?" That only compounds his sense of loss. He laments,

*These things I remember and I pour
out my soul within me.
For I used to go along with the throng
and lead them in procession to the house of God,*

With the voice of joy and thanksgiving,
a multitude keeping festival (v. 4).

Instead of folding under the pressure, his heart resists the temptation to fill his life with the empty promises of the local, temporal gods. His heart flies to God as the source of his sustenance.

Why are you in despair, O my soul?
And why have you become disturbed within me?
Hope in God, for I shall again praise Him
For the help of His presence (v. 5).

Some of us would say, theologically speaking, we are never alone. We believe God's presence is an entitlement bought by our redemptive transaction with Him. I concede the point. But that is *just* the point. Unlike the psalmist, we view God as a bag of tricks into which we can reach when life demands it. It's not that we don't relate to God at certain points. We are pleased to belong to God and to serve Him as opportunities arise. We are glad to obey God and live for Him. But to *long* for God seems not to be in our spiritual repertoire. We have learned to be *busy* for God without *needing* Him so deeply that we can't get enough of Him.

Yet not getting enough of Him is what belonging to Him is all about. To uncover and listen afresh to this call of our souls should be the focused pursuit of our lives. We can be positionally connected to Him and His resources but functionally alone in the ongoing experience of life. Then, when we suddenly need Him (though in reality He is always there and available), we find that because we have not cultivated an ongoing relationship with Him we don't know how to connect with Him and experience His support. We feel the sense of isolation and helplessness that is at the heart of aloneness.

INTIMACY: FOOD FOR OUR SOULS

The opposite of aloneness is intimacy. We normally think of intimacy in terms of close encounters of the personal kind. The intimacy offered by our shallow, sometimes shabby, society is cast in terms of apparel, one-night stands, colognes, video titles, evenings of candlelight and deep red wine, luxury cars, or voyeuristic exchanges on the Internet or in some smoke-filled nightclub.

This is not the intimacy our souls crave. Every time we dip into these buckets, we come up empty. The intimacy we long for is found in a growing relationship to the One who is perfectly suited to satisfy and sustain us. As we have seen, true intimacy is what we experience as we grow more deeply conscious of, connected to, and confident in Him and Him alone as our unfailing resource in life. It can't be purchased at the corner newsstand. Nor can it be pursued in the marketplace, on vacations, or through the hottest of social calendars. When it comes to intimacy, these are the small talk of life compared with the deep satisfaction that comes from profound interactions with the God who alone can fill our souls.

> *The intimacy we long for is found in a growing relationship to the One who is perfectly suited to satisfy and sustain us.*

When the Pharisees asked Christ what was the greatest commandment, He replied, "You shall love the Lord your God with all your heart, and with all your soul, and with all your mind, and with all your strength" (Mark 12:30; see also Deuteronomy 6:5; Matthew 22:37). He knew that a prioritized pursuit of God was the way in which life at its best would be realized and fulfilled.

When last we saw the Prodigal, he had cashed in his inheritance and started walking away from the intimacy of home and family. He didn't stop until he was far away. As his story continues, we learn that "he squandered his estate with loose living" (Luke 15:13). We aren't told exactly what was entailed. We later discover that the older brother assumed that prostitutes were involved, but perhaps that was sour-grapes speculation on his part.

The Prodigal simply went on a spending spree. But then again, maybe he was searching to capture a connectedness for which his soul longed. He could buy new stuff. He could buy new friends. He could even wear the title of Mr. Big Spender from Out of Town.

But when his circumstances took a turn for the worse, it all evaporated. "When he had spent everything, a severe famine occurred in that country, and he began to be impoverished" (Luke 15:14).

For the first time in his life, the Prodigal Son was learning what it was truly like to be "impoverished"—in need. When he was at home, his father was there to provide for him. Lately he had been able to simply cash in another CD from his inheritance. But now what could he do?

Self-sufficiency is life's greatest barricade to intimacy with God.

If we do not conscientiously pursue intimacy with God our Father, we will eventually find ourselves in this same dilemma.

The Prodigal's problem was that he thought his material and social world was sufficient. Self-sufficiency is life's greatest barricade to intimacy with God.

Why is it that prayer, real prayer, is such a scarce commodity among Christians? Why are we so biblically illiterate? Why do we find so little time to find God in His Word and seek guidance and counsel from Him? Why are we so quick to deny Him and His ways when life puts us to the test and forces a choice? Why do we so readily take the credit and bask in the glory of our own lives and accomplishments? Why are we not more grateful?

Why do we not live in adoring dependence on God?

Because we live connected to all the wrong stuff and feel that all that we have is sufficient. Self-sufficiency may be adequate for some things—up to a point. But when we get past that point, self-sufficiency crumbles. If we don't have a growing relationship with God, we're out of options.

IT'S NOT JUST THE STUFF

But not all of us are committed materialists. Some of us know that piles of stuff soon lose their capacity to thrill and fulfill. We may agree with Muhammad Ali, who used to "dance like a butterfly, sting like a bee." As a former athlete now crippled by Parkinson's disease, he reflected, "I had the world, and it wasn't nuthin'."[1] We may even be proud that we have escaped the clutches of consumerism—*we* cling to friends, family, and relationships. And admittedly, while those are far more satisfying (When was the last time you felt warmed and loved by hugging your new car?), the fact remains that relationships can be a source of deep disappointment. Attaching our expectations for the good life to the warm and huggy lane of relationships is risky indeed.

Friendships are often built on the common turf of career, sports, or political interests. When the reason for connecting is gone, so is the connection.

Granted, it's not always that friends are fickle. It's just that life has a way of making even loyal relationships distant. After we have poured all that we are and have into our children, they fall in love, build their own lives, and move away, leaving us feeling empty and alone. Life partners are taken in death after years of fulfilling intimacy, never to be replaced again. The best of lifelong friends can be transferred to the other side of the continent, where they start a new life without us.

One of the greatest shams in our generation is the idea that all the rewards of satisfaction, security, and sustenance can come from liberated sexual experiences. This generation has invested deeply into the notion that the rewards of intimacy can be had in a series of quick hits with a variety of sexual partners. But now even that hope has dimmed. One issue of *U.S. News & World Report* ran a cover story entitled "The Trouble with Premarital Sex." The subtitle made the point: "Americans Don't Think It's Too Much of a Problem. Maybe They Should." The article argued that the idea that sexual freedom delivers intimacy is a mistaken notion. Perhaps Jennifer Grossman, a thirty-year-old single woman and contributor for MSNBC-TV, gave the most telling statement in a sidebar interview entitled "Was It Good for Us?" Grossman, identified by the author as a self-described libertarian, said:

> I used to complain to my mother, who is a liberal, about how boyfriends seemed commitment shy. And she would say, "Well why buy the cow if the milk is free?" We're in the sexual promised land now, the milk is free, people are surfeited with sex— and yet we're starved for love . . . The safe-sex jingle—"You're

sleeping with everyone your lover has ever slept with"—has added resonance now: You're sharing emotional space with those ex-wives and the girlfriends... The acceptance, even encouragement of premarital sex makes it very difficult to sustain the fantasy that we are loved alone.[2]

Jennifer's musings are telling. Promiscuity promises everything and delivers very little. As she notes with such clarity, we have a deep desire in our souls to be loved exclusively, and the "sexual promised land" does not fulfill that need.

No doubt the oldest delusion is that what truly and ultimately satisfies and secures us is gaining honor, glory, power, and position. Satan was once a great and magnificent angel of light, but he wanted the honor, power, and personal glory due only to God. It was his heart's desire to displace God and assume the mantle of the glory of God. God judged him for this. Ever since, he has been actively urging humankind to taste the bitter fruit of its own folly.

A monologue spoken by Cardinal Wolsey in Shakespeare's *Henry VIII* puts earthly renown into perspective. The cardinal gained unparalleled power and influence during the king's reign. After years of wielding his personal leverage and basking in honor and influence, he became the victim of a treacherous plot crafted by his enemies and fell from the king's favor. Upon being stripped of his lofty credentials, he thinks rationally for the first time. Standing alone on stage, he delivers a soliloquy that profoundly declares a truth all of us need to hear.

"Farewell! A long farewell, to all my greatness," he begins.

One day, he says, we put forth the "tender leaves" of our hopes; the next day honors blossom thick upon us. But a third day comes, and a "killing frost . . . nips [the] root" of our greatness and we fall. At the height of his power, he floated down a "sea of glory" like boys bobbing on a river on floats. But now his "high-blown pride" has broken under him. He is left, as he says,

Weary and old with service, to the mercy
Of a rude stream, that must for ever hide me.

"Vain pomp and glory of this world, I hate ye," he cries out. "Oh, how wretched / Is that poor man that hangs on princes' favours!" They who depend upon the smiles of princes will "fall like Lucifer / Never to hope again" when the "sweet aspect" of the ruler turns against them.

Wolsey's servant Cromwell enters, inquiring about how the former powerful political figure is coping with the sudden collapse of the platform he once strode upon in glory. Wolsey replies:

> *Never so truly happy, my good Cromwell.*
> *I know myself now, and I feel within me*
> *A peace above all earthly dignities,*
> *A still and quiet conscience.*

In taking from his shoulders the seals of office, the king has cured him of much and has removed

> *A load would sink a navy—too much honour.*
> *O 'tis a burden, Cromwell, 'tis a burden*
> *Too heavy for a man that hopes for heaven!*[3]

Some of us assessed early on the risks of building our expectations on material good, social networks, fame, and fortune and decided not to venture into those territories. Either the circumstances of life prohibited us from making the attempt, or we made a conscious assessment that those fields of dreams were too risky. So we decided to travel to the interior of our own worlds and manage those environments in ways we believed would satisfy and sustain us and keep us safe. But a life focused on self is certain to bring on the emptiness of aloneness. The walls we erect to keep ourselves secure will only shield us from the resources God intends for our support.

DESIRING WHAT WE NEED

Meaningful relationships, large bank accounts, fully funded retirement plans, strong purchasing power, high organizational position, and the "right" social connections are not wrong in themselves or even to be shunned. Nor are good health and a sense of well being. God "richly supplies us with all things to enjoy" (1 Timothy 6:17). The flaw is to think that in them we can find ultimate satisfaction, sustenance, and security.

The issue is not that we have fixed our hope on wrong things but that we have fixed our hope on lesser things. Material and social benefits were never intended to serve us in the way that we hoped that they would, which is why the Bible warns us not to fix our hopes on them (1 Timothy 6:17).

> *The issue is not that we have fixed our hope on wrong things but that we have fixed our hope on lesser things.*

In Greek mythology, Tantalus was a king who revealed the gods' secrets to mortals. As punishment, he was placed in a river in Hades with water up to his chin. Just above his head was a tree with clusters of hanging fruit. But every time he attempted to drink from the river, the waters receded, and every time he tried to pick the ripe fruit, it rose just above his reach. He was doomed forever to suffer hunger, thirst, and unfulfilled desire. It is from this story that we get our word *tantalize*. It's hard to think of a better image for aloneness. If we reach for intimacy through material well being and social success and not through a relationship with God, we will never quite capture it.

This should concern us.

Striving for, clinging to, and hoping in all that is within our grasp displaces God from His rightful place in our lives. We were built for God. Only He can satisfy the vacancy in our souls. His nature, provision, power, and wisdom are the only realities that will unfailingly buttress our lives with that which truly sustains and secures.

God does not compete. Nor does He share space with anyone or anything. We either fix our hope on Him alone by cultivating a connected intimacy with and radical reliance upon Him, or we build our lives on the delusions that all we really need is what we can construct around ourselves from the resources at our earthly disposal.

four

IT HAPPENED IN EDEN

A History of Aloneness

THEY HEARD THE SOUND OF THE LORD GOD WALKING
IN THE GARDEN IN THE COOL OF THE DAY, AND THE MAN
AND HIS WIFE HID THEMSELVES FROM THE PRESENCE
OF THE LORD GOD AMONG THE TREES OF THE GARDEN.
—GENESIS 3:8

Of all the trying seasons of being a parent, one of the most difficult is the season when children interject the "W" word into every conversation.

"Why do dogs bark?"

"Why is the sky blue?"

"Why does our cat have whiskers?"

"Why does Grandpa snore?"

And since we usually don't know why, we respond with the "Just because" answer. Martie and I are blooming grandparents now and are bracing for another go-round with the "Why?" syndrome.

At this juncture, however, the question "Why?" is important. Why do we struggle with aloneness? How do we drift away from that intimate contact with Christ at the point of our redemption toward aloneness? It is hard to imagine that you can even get from intimacy to aloneness.

Is life some inside joke with a void at the center where nothing can be placed on deposit? Are emptiness and hopelessness part and parcel of the created purpose of life? Is this disconnected, vulnerable life the best that there is?

Thankfully, the answer is no to all of the above. There is an ultimate resource that guarantees satisfaction, sustenance, and security in the face of any circumstance of life. We simply need to link up with that resource and stay connected.

IN THE BEGINNING

The "Why?" question is put into context when we understand that the aloneness the Prodigal experienced—and we experience—has a history that began in Eden where Adam and Eve lived in the pleasure of a relationship connected to the fullness of God. They were fully satisfied and sustained. They were safe. And they were never alone. They had all they needed and more in God, each other, and the created order around them.

But then something catastrophic happened. What had satisfied and sustained them without disappointment or despair was stripped from them by a self-inflicted wound of personal aggrandizement. Their despair was rooted in the sudden sense of loss and aloneness that was in sharp contrast to the depth of completeness and intimacy they had enjoyed unhindered up to that point. Since that day life has never been the same. The catastrophic event in Eden cast the whole world and ensuing generations into a state of alienation and aloneness. Since that day aloneness has ruled and written history.

Let's go back and start from the beginning.

There is a reason we yearn for satisfaction and sustenance. Our need for these ingredients in a well-ordered and tranquil life is grounded in the way God built us. The impulse to find and embrace them comes from deep within our beings. If we tried to resign ourselves to ignoring them, none of us would be cynical or stoical enough to be happy in the loss. No wall of defense around us would be big enough or thick enough to quell the impulse of our desire for them.

Reconnecting begins with understanding the way it was in Eden.

In the beginning God had a plan for Himself and the people He would create, where He would put them, and how everything would work toward their maximum good and gain. It started with His desire to create humanity for His own pleasure and glory. After creating a splendid and perfectly supportive environment, His ultimate stroke in creation was Adam and Eve. And, unlike anything else He had created, he formed them in *His own image* (Genesis 1:27).

This is a critical part of understanding our struggle and finding our way back. Being created in the image of God does not mean that we look like God. It means that we are created to be compatible with Him. This compatibility enables us to connect with Him and His satisfying and stabilizing resources. It gives us the capacity to fulfill our created destiny to reflect Him so that He might be glorified through us.

How does being made in God's image enable us to connect?

God is a God of emotions, and we are created as emotional people. God is a God who has a will, and we are created with a will. God is a God of personality, and He has given us distinct personalities. God is a God who is intelligent, and He has created us with a capacity for intelligence. He is creative, and we reflect that in our creativity. He is a spirit, and we are made as spiritual beings.

God has done all of this so that we could connect with Him at every level. Intimacy is about His emotions becoming my emotions so that I love what He loves, hate what He hates, and enjoy what He enjoys. It's about His will becoming my will, His personality and character forming my personality and character, His mind and thoughts filling my mind and thoughts.

We are built for Him, and this compatibility makes connectability possible.

We are built for Him, and this compatibility makes connectability possible.

The fact that we were built to connect also guarantees that He, in all His fullness, can flow into us and fill our lives. In a sense, when He built us for Himself, He was guaranteeing that He was "built" for *us*. As we are compatible to Him, He is compatible to us. In the innermost parts of our being, where no one can interfere or disrupt, we can connect with all that He is. He fits into all the corners, cracks, and crannies of our souls. And all that He is able to transfer to us can be received and enjoyed. Being made in His image guarantees that we can experience the satisfying realities of His love, mercy, grace, presence, power, protection, justice, and comfort; and that we can absorb His wisdom and revel in who He is and who He is to us personally.

When we are committed in increasing measure, we find an increasing, in-depth, soulish satisfaction in the richness and security of sustaining experiences with Him. Seeking deep, intimate, ongoing satisfaction anywhere else will only disillusion us. We are built for Him, and our lives are always at their best when we experientially engage that reality in our lives.

So life didn't start as a meaningless, meandering experience in the face of the winds of fate. In the beginning Adam and Eve found purpose, worth, and prosperity in their unaltered connection to the fullness of their God. They were fully satisfied and sustained. They were safe and never alone. They had all they needed and more in God, each other, and the created order around them.

What they had is instructive in terms of what God intends for us if we are to be intimately satisfied in Him and through Him.

TRUSTED RELATIONSHIPS

After each created act God stepped back and concluded that "it was good" (Genesis 1:10, 12, 18, 21, 25, 31). No doubt the angels sang a thousand Hallelujah Choruses each time to affirm how impressed they were. But when He looked at Adam, who was the only animate part of the creation without another being like him, God's assessment was, "It is *not good* that man should be alone" (2:18 NKJV, emphasis added). Even though Adam had an unhindered relationship to the fullness of God, there was a sense in which he was not complete without a trusted relationship to another human being. It was not God's intention for Adam to be humanly alone, even if he was spiritually fulfilled. So God created a complementing source of fulfillment and fellowship through whom He could satisfy and sustain Adam—something with "skin" on it.

I have often wanted to jump into a time capsule and watch from the bushes as God put Adam to sleep and created Eve from his side. Imagine Adam's first glance out of his groggy recovery. I doubt if there has ever been a more exhilarating moment in the history of humanity than the moment that Adam first laid eyes on Eve. She was made like him, yet wonderfully different. Together they had the created capacity to communicate, to share life on the same wavelength, and to participate in life's endeavors with a compatibility that would connect them intimately in each aspect of life. Together they would be satisfied and sustained, not just in their own relationship but also in their mutual connectedness to their God.

THE PLEASURE OF PROPERTY

The created order around them would be an additional source of satisfaction and sustenance. God provided the garden of Eden as a place where they would know the joy of keeping it and subduing it for His glory (Genesis 1:26–31). It would be a place where Adam and Eve could demonstrate their unflinching devotion to God as they maintained the garden and obeyed His instructions for life within its boundaries. It would never satisfy or sustain by itself. Only in the context of their connectedness to God and each other would the material order have meaning and significance.

This, then, is life as it was meant to be. An unhindered trust and confidence in an all-sufficient God, the enjoyment of intimate fellowship in an earthly trusted relationship, and the pleasures of an abundant environment to support them—all within the context of a glad and obedient priority relationship to the God who created and gave it all to them.

God has abundantly blessed me. I have had the privilege of knowing and fellowshipping with many good and interesting people. I have traveled much of the world and experienced life widely and deeply. I have been blessed with many comforts and, like many, have acquired material goods that are fun and fleetingly fulfilling. And while there have been bumps in the road, I really couldn't ask for more. But I know in the depths of my own spirit that if all I had in life were material things and my experiences, my life would be flat compared with the satisfying and sustaining pleasure I have found in a connected devotion to God and in the trusted relationships He has provided for me. And while these deeper, more fulfilling ingredients have sometimes faltered in the intrigue of the world around me and in the business of life, I am never more satisfied and sustained than when my connectedness to God and the people I love is building momentum in my life.

In fact, all the good stuff in the material order takes on a more dramatic dimension when we are enjoying intimacy with God and others. Our possessions and experiences provide periodic frosting on the cake, but if the sweetness of the frosting is not all I had expected it to be, the true nourishment of my life remains intact.

The greatest day in the office, the most exciting evening at the ballpark, the best meal I've had in a long time, that meaningful kiss, and even the best golf shot I've hit all year are fuller, richer experiences because my relationship to God and to the few who are close to me are the truly significant parts of my life.

> *If I don't believe I need Him, I probably won't desire Him.*

If my work at the office goes south on me or if my golf game is in the ditch—as unsettling as these circumstances might be—with God and Martie as my closest experienced pleasures, the day at the office and the horrendous golf score aren't nearly as devastating. I wasn't looking to them for real satisfaction and sustenance anyway.

And if something happens to a trusted relationship, I still have the stability and unlimited resources of my God to get me through. Even if I *feel* alone and cry myself to sleep, I am not alone.

Peter Kreeft's words ring true in my heart: "The world's purest gold is only dung without Christ. But with Christ, the basest metal is transformed into the purest gold . . . With him, poverty is riches, weakness is power, suffering is joy, to be despised is glory. Without him, riches are poverty, power is impotence, happiness is misery, glory is despised."[1]

This was God's plan in the beginning. We would be built for Him, and He would not only find pleasure in us but also be pleased to satisfy us with all that He is and to sustain us with all that His matchless wealth could release on our behalf. And while He is all-sufficient in Himself, He has chosen to channel His provision our way through the gifts of trusted human relationships and the material order.

> *He has chosen to channel His provision our way through the gifts of trusted human relationships and the material order.*

The whole scheme is built to operate in an unalterable sequence. It is structured to begin with God as the preeminent, present, pleasurable center of it all. Our relationships to one another are to be experienced in the context of His presence and guidance. And the world around us is to be a means whereby He can provide all things for us to enjoy while we in turn use our lives and His gifts to worship, serve, and glorify Him with gratitude and obedience.

This is how it was in Eden.

Life was good.

Life was satisfying, and Adam and Eve were fully sustained.

And they were never alone.

Never.

But then something happened. Something horrible happened. It was profound in its far-reaching damage. What happened in Eden touches us today at the depths of our souls. It is an event from which none of us have fully recovered. It explains why we are haunted with aloneness.

ALONENESS: A HISTORY

In Genesis 3 the Enemy shows up to strike a devastating blow to the Edenic experience of unlimited satisfying and sustaining intimacy. In fact, the history of the Enemy reveals that he himself is suffering like no other from an intense depth of aloneness, having been banished from the presence of God (Isaiah 14:12–15). Could it be that Satan now comes into God's perfectly created arrangement to impose upon humanity the same affliction that plagues his own soul? If that was his aim, he was eminently successful.

Satan said to Eve, "Did God really say, 'You must not eat from any tree in the garden'?" (Genesis 3:1 NIV). Actually God had told Adam and Eve that they could eat of *all* the trees except *one*. But now the Alone One has crafted the question in such a way as to give Eve the impression that God was being restrictive and oppressive.

This subtle deceit was the trash talk that began to drive a wedge between Eve and her unqualified connectedness to God. By getting Eve to doubt God's goodness, Satan kicked the door open to the second disconnecting impression—the inference that life would be more meaningful, satisfying, and sustaining if she had unrestricted access to the world around her, even if it meant disconnecting from God. God plus all that He had put in her legitimate reach would not be enough. After all, Satan suggested, God was the One who wanted to hold her back. Surely she could find complete satisfaction and sustenance in the created order around her.

What is important to note here is that Eve didn't commit an act of blatant denial of God. She simply came to believe that *He wasn't enough for her.* The disaster that was about to happen was motivated by the belief that she could find more satisfaction in herself and the created order around her than in God. God wasn't enough. Nor was Adam. The important thing in life would be herself and her surroundings. As the text says, "When the woman saw that the tree was good for food" (sustenance), "and that it was a delight to the eyes" (satisfaction), "and that the tree was desirable to make one wise" (security), "she took from its fruit and ate" (v. 6).

God had already offered her all the sustenance, satisfaction, and security she could ever need, but she traded it away for what she thought would be *more.* In her shortsighted exchange Eve was like the dog in the fable who, carrying a juicy steak across a bridge, looked in the water and saw his reflection. Thinking it was another dog with a better steak, he lunged to snatch the other steak and got neither.

SEEING CLEARLY

This early moment in history unmasked the strategy of the tormented adversary who seeks to enlist us in his own misery. His strategy was to seduce Eve and subsequently Adam into believing two lies:

- that God is not generous and good but rather oppressive and restrictive
- that life is best and most expansively enjoyed when self is at the center, seeking satisfaction and sustenance in the material order, regardless of God's counsel and command

These twisted notions ushered aloneness into our world. They lay the groundwork for the aloneness that haunts our own existence today.

Eve wanted to be on her own. She wanted to be left alone to do it her way.

She got her wish—she was alone.

Alone as she had never been before.

The first clue that she had lost the blessings of satisfaction and intimacy came when she turned to Adam to give the forbidden fruit to him. If being alone was truly the source of satisfaction and sustenance Satan cracked it up to be, she would have kissed both God and Adam goodbye. In fact, it is a clue to the depth of intimacy Adam and Eve had enjoyed in the garden that Adam took and ate, lest he lose her and his life return to the way it was before she was given as a gift to him.

> *Eve fell into aloneness by the allure of the creation around her.*

And here was the second blow. Though willing to compromise his relationship with God to keep his fulfilling and trusted relationship with Eve, when faced with the need to protect himself from danger, Adam put his friend in harm's way to preserve himself. When God confronted him, he blamed Eve to get himself off the hook. The coward said to God, "The *woman* whom You gave to be with me, *she* gave me from the tree, and I ate" (v. 12, emphasis added). So much for the bedrock of trusted relationships.

In a flash of disconnectedness, loyalty toward God and mutual trust toward each other were gone. Only self was important in the new order. For Adam and Eve, there was no humble honesty toward their God and no commitment to one another. Even the alliance Eve formed with the Enemy was expendable, as Eve pointed the finger of blame toward the Serpent (v. 13). And much to their dismay, the man and woman found that the world around them became a ghetto as they were banished from its pleasure to live in a cursed creation.

Adam's self-deception was that intimacy with people is of greater value than intimacy with God.

While Eve fell into aloneness by the allure of the creation around her, Adam's self-deception was that intimacy with people is of greater value than intimacy with God. Adam was the first of a long line of humanity who have been willing to deny allegiance to God in order to gain or keep a sense of connectedness to a person who has become a significant source of satisfaction and security.

But instead of satisfaction, Adam and Eve were overcome by a sense of isolation and shame. They were now in the far country and deeply felt the loss.

MEASURING THE LOSS

Instead of enhancing their existence, Adam and Eve's disconnection from God left them disenfranchised and alone—alienated from five life-enriching points of connectedness.

- God Himself as personal friend, provider, and satisfier
- The moral guidance that God provides as a directing and defining influence that keeps us from danger and guarantees prosperity
- Trusted relationships with other people through whom God supplies portions of His satisfaction and sustenance
- The untainted enjoyment of the material world as a provision from God rather than a replacement of God

- Hope and confidence in a bright and secure future

Their breach of intimacy with God created a stark sense of isolation in their souls.

- Self was now the source of satisfaction.
- Personal authority supplanted obedience to the rules and guiding principles God gave human beings so that they would experience safe and prosperous lives.
- Suspicion and cynicism undergirded by a lack of trust in others became the norm.
- The material order would now dominate the attention and focus of humanity's work and wealth.
- Fear, hopelessness, pessimism, and ultimately despair took over, as disconnectedness from God produced a deepening aloneness in their souls.

All of life would now be managed by these new rules, and all who would want to go it on their own would ultimately know the pain and despair that Satan feels. The world became more crowded, sophisticated, intellectually acute, and affluent; but with the new rules in place, humanity became increasingly alone.

The Enemy no doubt slithered back into hell with a sinister sense of joy when he left Adam and Eve. He knew that the garden without God could not satisfy them. He knew that without God they could not satisfy each other. He knew that he himself would not satisfy or sustain them—indeed, he *couldn't*. So he left them alone.

The barrier between Adam and Eve and God was huge. When Adam and Eve "heard the sound of the LORD God walking in the garden in the cool of the day" (Genesis 3:8), instead of running to Him, seeking to be forgiven and restored, they hid, covered by the fig leaves of their own efforts to recover what they had lost. They now lived in shame and knew the agony of alienation from the most important entity in their existence.

Yet in the midst of this loss of intimacy and the arrival of aloneness, it is significant to note that God took the initiative and walked back into the garden. If we didn't know the story and tried to imagine what might happen next, we might have imagined God exercising a host of options. He could have annihilated everything and started over again. He could have ignored Adam and Eve and let them live with the consequences of rejecting Him, allowing their new scheme of existence to run its degenerative course. Or He could do the unexpected. He could restore the relationship they had so carelessly given up. He could call them back to Himself and to a consistent moral order that would again make possible intimacy with Him and the development of trusted relationships.

He loves us because He is love and because He created us for the pleasure of our fellowship and the ultimate glory of His name.

And that is just what He did. It is all the more surprising when we realize that God is the only entity in the universe who can be alone and be fully satisfied and sustained. It may come as a blow to us that God does not need us! But the beauty of it is that even though He can go for eternity without us, He chooses to love us and care for us, which makes His love and concern for us richer still. He doesn't love us for what it will do for Him. Too many of us have been wounded by that kind of love. He loves us because He *is* love and because He created us for the pleasure of our fellowship and the ultimate glory of His name. It was that kind of love and compassion that drove Him to seek to reconnect Adam and Eve to Himself.

He offers the same privilege to us today.

He is driven by a divine desire to reconnect with those who have fallen for the hollow promises of the Enemy. That was the purpose of the cross. For in the cross, our sin, which separated us, is dealt with. If we trust and repentantly embrace the Savior, we are restored—not by our merits but by His surpassing grace (Ephesians 2:8–9). In fact, God's plan throughout history has been to bring this about. Scripture opens with intimacy in perfect sequence as God satisfies and sustains those He created. As we shall see, Scripture closes with an eternal restoration of intimacy with those whom He has gathered to Himself—only by then the Enemy will be eternally banished. We will have no fear of ever being separated from God again.

But until then we live in constant jeopardy of falling prey to what is often a slow and subtle drift from God.

A PRODIGAL'S PROGRESS

When we disconnect from God, even in small ways, it usually is to attach to something else. The Prodigal disconnected from his father for the allure of the far country and subsequently faced personal disaster. We are told, "He went and hired himself out to one of the citizens of that country" (Luke 15:15). He had known the joy of a fine and trusted relationship with his father. He had also known the reckless and exciting life away from home as long as it was bankrolled by his share of Dad's estate. But now he would know hard work, indentured servanthood, and slavery.

We may find ourselves in a similar situation if we don't learn to detect the symptoms of aloneness at an early stage. And more essential than *detecting* the symptoms is doing something to eliminate them and rekindle intimacy with God. Like the Prodigal, we might not be alarmed to discover we're far from home—not if we assume we have the resources to meet all our needs. But to discover ourselves far from home *and* flat broke *and* alone—that's a stark reality that makes us long for home.

five

DRIFTING AWAY FROM GOD

Six Steps of Separation

IT IS BETTER TO FAIL IN A CAUSE THAT WILL
ULTIMATELY SUCCEED THAN TO SUCCEED
IN A CAUSE THAT WILL ULTIMATELY FAIL.
—PETER MARSHALL

Tom is a guy who can't swim but nevertheless enjoys a vacation at the beach. On a recent trip he was casually bobbing around on a float just offshore. He closed his eyes, basking in the warm sun and enjoying the soft, rolling waves that undulated beneath his raft. When he opened his eyes, to his shock the shore was considerably farther away than it had been before. He hopped off the float to get back to the security of the sand, only to realize that the water was over his head.

Panicked, he quickly scrambled back aboard his small rubber raft. The current had carried him away from anyone he knew, so he couldn't get their attention with hand signals. No one else was in the water nearby. The people on the beach were yelling and having fun, so he didn't think anyone would hear his shouting for help. (Besides, he was a bit embarrassed to be in this predicament.) He decided to hang on and inch his way toward shore bit by bit with each wave. His progress was slow and scary, but he made it.

The drift of our lives away from God is just as subtle. And it is frightening to wake up to find that we're not only far from where we should be but also way over our heads.

What is it that sets us adrift? From the lives of the first people in Genesis, we can identify six characteristics of a point of departure from an intimate relationship with God. Read the list. Check it twice. Measure where you are in these steps away from God.

1. Doubting God's goodness, wisdom, and the perfection of His intentions toward us

When Satan wanted to break the bond of intimacy between Eve and God, he didn't try to deny the existence of God blatantly. She had had too much personal contact with Him for that to work. Instead Satan started where he usually starts—by driving a wedge between Eve and her trust in and affection for God. There was no way she would fall for the fruit unless Satan could get her to doubt that God was good and to question whether God had her best intentions in mind when He restricted her from eating of the tree of the knowledge of good and evil.

Satan breaks our trust in God by getting us to interpret God, His Word, and our life experiences in non-truthful ways. By the time Eve abandoned God for the supposed benefits of her world, nothing about God had changed. All that had changed was her interpretation of the facts she had previously lived with in glad submission. The generous God who had given her and Adam everything in the garden but *one* tree she now saw as stingy and restrictive, keeping her from something she desired to bring her satisfaction. Worse, Satan suggested, He was selfishly preventing her from sharing in His great knowledge and power.

Once we begin to suspect God instead of respecting and honoring Him, we have begun the trek away from Him. Life is full of scenarios where Satan can steal our affection for God by putting his deceitful twist on our experiences. We must remember that he is the spin doctor of hell and—as Christ said—the father of lies (John 8:44). Watch for these distorted thoughts:

- Blaming God for the evil Satan has inspired and superimposed on our lives
- Perceiving God as a God who has been good to others but has denied us position, pleasure, or prosperity and drawing the conclusion that God is not good to us

- Feeling that we have been good but that God has used us and not rewarded us, leaving our righteousness an empty sacrifice
- Being blinded to the fact that God can take the worst things in our lives and orchestrate them for good and gain
- Becoming convinced that God's ways and His will for us are unduly restrictive and oppressive

Fewer moments in history are more graphic in their display of this tension between our experience and our view of God than the interchange between Job and his wife. Both of them had plenty of reason to see life from Satan's point of view. Job's children were dead, his fortune was gone, and his health was destroyed. His wife, whose heart had been turned against God by her shared tragedy with Job, counseled him: "Curse God and die!" (Job 2:9). Job's perspective? "Though He slay me, I will hope in Him" (13:15). Same circumstances. Two different thought patterns. Job had an intimate connection with God that could not be broken by life's circumstances, no matter how wrenching. The tougher life got, the more he felt he needed God. And, as Peter Kreeft points out, in God "Job has everything even though he has nothing," in contrast to the godless person, who has "nothing even though he has everything."[1]

The writer of Psalm 27 reflects the same confidence as he embraces God in the midst of calamities:

Though a host encamp against me,
My heart will not fear;
Though war arise against me,
In spite of this I shall be confident . . .
For in the day of trouble He will conceal me in His tabernacle;
In the secret place of His tent He will hide me;
He will lift me up on a rock (vv. 3, 5).

We can defend ourselves against the pressure to abandon God by remembering just a few truths:

- Satan is our enemy and seeks to destroy us by alienating us from the only resource that can support and sustain us (1 Peter 5:8).

- It is Satan rather than God who is not good and who has ill intentions against us (John 8:44; 1 Peter 5:8).
- Though God permits all that comes into our lives, evil is perpetrated by Satan and as such he—not God—deserves the blame for initiating ill-motivated actions against us (Job 1).
- God permits negative events in our lives only when He can in time turn them to His glory, the advance of the kingdom, and our good (Romans 8:28).
- God's laws and principles are good. They are intended to keep us out of harm's way and to direct us in ways that will ultimately bless and prosper us (Psalm 1).
- The most powerful statement we can make to a watching world is to assert by word and deed that our God is worthy of our affection and allegiance even when we ride through storms and do not seem to be as blessed as others (Job 2:10; Acts 5:41; 16:19–25).

The discipline of unwavering trust in God will keep us close to home. No one deserves this kind of allegiance more than God, who cares intensely for us and does all things well.

2. Believing that we need more than God and what He has provided to satisfy, sustain, and secure our lives

The issue here does not deny the fact that God does meet our needs through secondary means. Rather it lies in assuming that the secondary stuff in and of itself is what we need, even if getting it requires that we become disloyal to God.

That was the sense of the message the Enemy sent to Eve. "To continue to be completely loyal to God will result in your life being less than it could be—in fact, less than it *should* be. What He has permitted is not only manipulatively restrictive, it just plain isn't enough. Your life could be richer, more satisfying, and more complete if you were not bound by loyalty to Him and His rules."

Stepping across the line of love and loyalty to God for these reasons is a temptation that is almost more than we can resist. Satan stands like an auctioneer, mesmerizing us with the cadence of his call to have what he offers, to have more than God has permitted. But, like Eve, every time we step across the line and reach for the forbidden fruit, we lose. We lose intimacy with God, peace of mind, a clean conscience, and confidence in ourselves to know and to do what is right. Instead of inheriting blessings, we inherit guilt, shame, and fear of the future.

Satan will use this wedge to separate us from our God in any arena of our lives; for Satan, nothing is exempt. In our business we are urged to be less than righteous to gain more on the bottom line. Would we deny God for a raise? for a promotion? for the thrill of the kill in a competitive struggle for that coveted contract? for bragging rights about the size of our company or the price of our stock? Would we give less of our income to God than is appropriate so that we have more to spend on ourselves? Would we deny our loyalty to Him for the quick hits and adrenaline rush of pleasures that are out of bounds?

In the account of Moses in Hebrews 11, we read that he valued his relationship to God even more than personal comfort, position, and prosperity: "By faith Moses . . . refused to be called the son of Pharaoh's daughter, choosing rather to endure ill-treatment with the people of God than to enjoy the passing pleasures of sin, considering the reproach of Christ greater riches than the treasures of Egypt" (Hebrews 11:24–26). We all must eventually figure out what the "Egypt" is in our lives and measure it against the unsurpassable riches of knowing and relating to Christ intimately.

3. Placing meaningful relationships above loyalty to God

At the close of a large men's breakfast in suburban Chicago, a man in his late forties approached me and said that as a result of what he had heard at the breakfast, there was a new flame in his heart to become God's kind of man. He went on to say, however, that he had been having an affair for the last several years and doubted that he would ever really want to break that off.

There are times in our lives when we have to make strategic choices about relationships. For this gentleman, the choice was clear. If he were to have a growing relationship with God, he would have to sever his relationship with this woman.

Adam's choice was clear as well. Think about the weight of that moment in the garden when—knowing that Eve had already stepped over the line of love and loyalty to God—he had to make a personal choice. There's no doubt that that choice was complicated by the same urgings in his own soul that had drawn Eve over the line. *What have I been missing out on by not eating of this tree?* There was the allure of curiosity and the assumption that things might indeed be better over there with her than with only God in the garden. But the compelling issue was that if he chose not to eat, he would lose Eve. And then he would be left alone again with God. And so Adam reached and ate and chose Eve over God.

All of us face this same tension throughout our lives. Meaningful, trusted relationships bring affirmation, a sense of worth, companionship, the pleasure of long walks together, and deep conversations that bond our spirits as one. We find in relationships what we've been looking for. Relationships provide measures of satisfaction, sustenance, and security for us emotionally, spiritually, intellectually, and physically—in fact, in every way. And the person with whom we are relating packages all of that for us. It is traumatic to think of giving up such a treasured benefit so that we can continue our personal walk with God.

But isn't this just the point? A deep and intimate walk with God proves that He alone can finally satisfy, sustain, and secure us. Do we trust Him enough to believe that He desires to provide the resources that will chase aloneness into the shadows? That He will ultimately provide, whether through Him in a deepening intimacy with Himself or through a legitimate, trusting relationship with a person He has provided? If God had provided Adam the marvelous gift of Eve, would He not have been able to do so again? Or even if God didn't, could Adam be so intensely loyal to God that he would trust God and live for Him even if God did not choose to reward him with another relationship?

The bottom line in beating the strategy of seductive relationships is having the unshakable conviction that God is the source of satisfaction, sustenance, and security. We will never decrease the distance we have allowed to develop between God and ourselves until we firmly and finally believe that God will ultimately and finally provide for our needs in His way and His time. When we come to believe that and make it a life conviction, this weapon in Satan's arsenal will be rendered useless.

Jim Elliot, who was martyred for his commitment to Christ on a sandy beach along the edge of the Curaray River in the dense rain forests of Ecuador in 1956, had come to the place in his life where his relationship to God was first and foremost. How else could he have gone to that beach with his four friends, knowing that this attempt to follow Christ in winning savage hearts for heaven might take from them not only their wives, children, and friends but their very lives?

> *We will never decrease the distance we have allowed to develop between God and ourselves until we firmly and finally believe that God will ultimately and finally provide for our needs in His way and His time.*

Long before he decided to take the gospel into the face of death, Jim wrote a letter to his parents from college about his view of dating and finding a wife. He decided to pursue his relationship with Christ and not be distracted until Christ provided the right woman. Speaking of Adam in the garden, he wrote: "He waited 'til God saw his need. Then God made Adam sleep, prepared for his mate, and brought her to him. We need more of this 'being asleep' in the will of God. Then we can receive what He brings us in His own time if at all."[2]

4. Conforming God and His worship to our wants and expectations

I'm convinced that Satan doesn't mind at all if we're religious, just so we are not religious according to the will and ways of God. Religion that is according to God, His will, and His ways is a matter of full allegiance. God doesn't share the platform of worship with anyone or anything else. True worship is never choreographed by our own whims and desires but rather is shaped by the truth and the Spirit, according to all that is fitting to bring before a worthy God.

Satan often works as a counterfeit. His goal is to reconfigure religion to cloud our view of God or close the road of accessibility to Him. Several years ago, thirty-nine intelligent, capable Americans committed mass suicide out of a desire to rise to the next level in their search for God by joining up with a spaceship exploring the depths of heaven. My heart grieves for those thirty-nine who drugged themselves to death, thinking they were on a journey to meet God, when in reality they were going to wake up on the other side to find that they had been deeply and horribly deceived.

Those of us who have come to God in legitimate and biblical ways marvel at the weird religious stuff we see going on around us. But we too have vulnerabilities in this arena. Sure, we have come to God through Jesus Christ, admitting that we are sinners, repenting of our sins, and seeking to make Him the Lord of our lives. We believe in heaven, we believe in hell, and we believe that God is righteous and just. But we still have a propensity to wear worship as a mask that covers sin in our lives that we are unwilling to release. It is easy for us to worship God on the outside while stubbornly keeping territory from Him on the inside.

This tendency is part of the problem Adam and Eve's son Cain had in his dealings with God. Martie and I have been sharing Christ with a neighbor of ours, and in the process a mutual friend gave this neighbor a Bible and a study guide that would guide her through the reading of Scripture. The next time we saw her, she told us that she wasn't reading the Bible any more because she couldn't understand why God would be so unfair as to accept Abel's sacrifice and reject Cain's. "After all," she said, "he was a farmer and simply brought to God what he had. Did God expect him to buy a different kind of sacrifice that would have been acceptable?"

She missed the point. It was not what Cain brought as a sacrifice that was displeasing to God but the fact that Cain's worship of God was a sham. It masked an unrighteous attitude that refused a fully devoted response to God.

We don't fully understand the problem of Cain until we grasp the New Testament's comments on it. In Hebrews 11:4, we read that the difference between Cain and Abel was that Abel was a righteous man and Cain was not. The distinction between the two men had to do with the kind of lives they were living, not the quality of sacrifices they brought. Jude's language is even more graphic when he writes about outwardly religious people who use religious activities to cover the reality of their sinful lives: "Woe to them! For they have gone the way of Cain" (v. 11). These people live without the fear of God in their lives, Jude says. They care only for themselves, flaunting the emptiness of their shame. They are grumblers, faultfinders, people who follow after their own lusts; they are arrogant and manipulative (vv. 11–16).

When Christ was here He had broad tolerance for sinners who were seeking healing but zero tolerance for the hypocrisy of religious folk who thought they had no need of healing. He pulled no punches in pointing it out and expressing His disdain. Jesus said that before we come to the altar we need to lay down all the gifts that we are bringing and make right any offenses we have committed against other people (Matthew 5:23–24).

In the Old Testament, after King Saul had specifically disobeyed God's order and then brought a sacrifice, the Lord told him through Samuel, "To obey is better than sacrifice" (1 Samuel 15:22).

The psalmist says,

Who may ascend into the hill of the LORD?
And who may stand in His holy place?
He who has clean hands and a pure heart,
Who has not lifted up his soul to falsehood
And has not sworn deceitfully (24:3–4).

The psalmist then goes on to say of these clean, clearly focused followers, "This is the generation of those who seek Him, who seek Your face" (v. 6).

We can serve God our whole lives as elders, Bible teachers, Sunday school teachers, kingdom philanthropists, counselors, missionaries, pastors, or college presidents. We can be emotionally charged as we sing exhilarating songs of worship in grand and glorious cathedral settings or highly energized praise rallies. We can give sacrificially of our financial resources to God. We can be touched by great preaching and even weep over lost and despairing sinners. But it is all a show if unhindered pursuit of God is not at the center of our lives. God doesn't want our busyness; He wants our hearts. That's why Christ reproved the Pharisees: "This people honors Me with their lips, but their heart is far away from Me" (Matthew 15:8).

God doesn't want our busyness; He wants our hearts.

The essence of worship of God is that it expresses God's worth and value. In fact, the English word *worship* comes from the concept of "worth-ship." True worship is the expression of the worthiness of someone. Worship of God expresses that He is more worthy than anything else in our lives, that He is *supremely* worthy. Worship finds ways to express that adoration. We tell God how worthy He is when we serve Him, listen to His Word, give of our resources to Him—and when we without qualification or equivocation obey Him.

One of the greatest expressions of how much we value God is when we demonstrate by our actions that He takes priority over plans and dreams and is worth more than the sin that allures us. When we are tempted, we have the marvelous opportunity to say to Him that He is worth more than the strong pull of our lusts. When we say no to temptation, it is a loud and clear expression of the worth of God in our lives. It is an act of worship.

That's what makes the mask of worship so distasteful to God. Instead of using our activities to express His worth, we use them to hide our shame. This issue goes to the core. Sin separates us from God, regardless of the outward appearance of our lives. There is no hope of drawing near to Him as long as we are clinging to our sin.

Hypocrisy is in a sense idolatry. Refusing to release sin and be cleansed means that we count our sin to be of greater worth than our relationship to God. We need to remember that God is a jealous God—and rightly so! He is the supreme God of the universe and has the right to be first in the league of our lives, to rule our lives without rival. If this right is threatened by flat-out sin or by putting secondary things above Him, we have become idolatrous.

One of the struggles missionaries face in Japan is that the culture is so polytheistic that people don't have the concept of a single God to be worshiped above all others. Many Japanese are happy to make Jesus Christ their God—except that in their minds they're just adding one more god to an already crowded god-shelf in their homes. We too are capable of claiming God as our God while we are still controlled and driven by the worship of other gods.

5. *Resisting His reproofs*

When we cling to the sin in our lives, God will be working every angle to make us aware of it and bring sufficient pressure to cause us to repent. God is not just a jealous God. He is a loving and caring God who does not want us to taste the destruction sin always brings. He wants us to know the joy of drawing close to Him, and He knows that sin destroys the potential for that intimacy. The writer of Proverbs tells us, "Whom the LORD loves He reproves, even as a father the son in whom he delights" (Proverbs 3:12).

Before Cain murdered Abel, God used reproofs to make Cain aware of the path he was treading. There was no hope of an ongoing relationship with God as long as he continued to maintain sin in his life (Genesis 4:5). God came again to Cain, pointing out that he was not doing well and offering him the opportunity to repent and come to God on His terms (vv. 6-7). Again, Cain rejected the reproof. At this point it was clear that Cain was committed to living life his own way and would not be responsive to the increasing pressure God was bringing to bear on his life.

Anyone who truly desires to draw close to God needs to live in an ongoing sensitivity to the reproofs of God in his life. These reproofs are both *internal* and *external*.

One internal reproof is the voice of God's Spirit. This almost always arrives immediately when we contemplate committing or have committed a sin. It's the spiritual *tilt* when we have violated the rules in the pinball game of life. We've all heard that still—and sometimes not-so-still—small voice telling us that we've been wrong and calling us back to God.

Shame is another internal reproof. Shame is the immediate loss of a sense of worth and dignity. Our adversary loves to use sin to erode the spiritually appropriate confidence we have in ourselves as people of worth and dignity created in the image of God. When we allow sin to corrupt the quality of that image, the immediate result is shame.

There is the inner reproof of guilt. Guilt is the alarm that rings in our souls with a clanging irritation until we deal with it. Unfortunately many of us try to deal with the reproof of guilt with weak rationalizations. "I couldn't help myself." "Everybody's doing it." "I owed it to myself." "One little slip isn't all that big a deal." "God will forgive me anyway."

All of these internal reproofs rob us of the peace, tranquillity, confidence, and security that intimacy with God provides. They are signals from God that something drastic has happened that needs immediate attention.

The Old Testament story of Jonah tells of a series of external reproofs God sets in motion to bring the prophet back into obedience to Him. Initially Jonah was at peace with himself in his rebellion against God. He flat out did not want to go to Nineveh and had so rationalized his rebellion that once he got on the boat to Tarsus he fell sound asleep. He slept so deeply that even a storm that threatened the safety of the ship did not wake him. Internal reproofs had lost their capacity to create in him the restlessness that would drive him to repentance and obedience.

Since internal reproofs had not taken hold of Jonah's heart, God used a storm, a pagan ship captain, the "coincidence" of the roll of the dice that pointed the finger of blame at him, the embarrassment of having to give a testimony about his supposed allegiance to God, and three days and three nights in a sleazy underwater hotel to bring Jonah back into obedience.

God has a host of ways to bring external pressure to bear on our lives to draw us back to Himself. It may be the presence of godly people whose lives radiate with character and closeness to God. It may be a communion service. It may be a sermon preached to a packed church that makes us feel totally exposed, as though all the lights but one were turned off and the preacher's words shone on us like a spotlight. It may be the public failure of another person and the clear consequences that have fallen on his or her life. As we view the proceedings, we may feel pressure to cleanse our own lives from similar sins lest the consequences fall upon us as well. It may be something our children say to us as they note an inconsistency or hypocrisy in our lives. It may even be a spouse or close friend who is willing to point out a particular problem in our lives. Or it may be the painful experience of being the brunt of criticism, where God may use even an enemy to act as a mirror to reveal what we truly are.

> *Reproofs are like a hall of mirrors, making it impossible for us to escape the reality of who we really are and how we really look to God.*

Reproofs are like a hall of mirrors, making it impossible for us to escape the reality of who we really are and how we really look to God. They are like the bathroom mirror that reminds us every morning that we desperately need a fix. As long as we are looking in the mirror, we are driven to do something about our disheveled condition.

6.   *Eliminating righteous reminders from our lives*

When Steve Jones won the U.S. Open in 1996, an irritated journalist wrote this of the victory:

> Jones paid tribute to another source of inspiration—his religion. An avowed Christian, he was playing with Lehman, another Christian, and, somewhat to his surprise, Lehman turned to him on the first green and said: "Steve, God wants us to be strong and courageous, for that is the will of the Lord." Lehman said something similar on the 16th hole, too.[3]

The story censured Jones and Lehman. "Aside from expressing the old-fashioned concept that one player can encourage a rival, one has to say that the flaunting of God and religion is becoming wearing." The author concluded, "One does not know Jones' shoe, hat or glove size, nor the state of his bank account. Do we need to know his religion?"[4] These reflections were not written in a personal opinion editorial but rather in a lead article in the *Times*, Great Britain's leading daily.

Do you ever wonder why the people least tolerated in our culture are those of us who believe that there is a right and a wrong and a God who will ultimately judge the rebellion mirrored in the lives of men? This seems an odd bias in a culture that values tolerance above all else. But there is a good reason for it: an unrighteous society is uncomfortable when righteous reminders confront it.

When Cain refused to heed the reproofs of God, the only way he could cope with his choice was to eliminate the things in his environment that reminded him of his failure. Abel was the first target. Cain's instinctive response has become an ongoing pattern in our own culture of hostility and intolerance toward symbols and proclamations of righteousness.

But it's not just a dynamic in our culture. Once we start to drift toward the far country, we too show the tendency to separate ourselves from reminders of home. Howard Hendricks of Dallas Theological Seminary's Center for Christian Leadership surveyed 246 ministers who had fallen in their ministries due to moral failure. As reported by Steve Farrar in *Finishing Strong*, Hendricks found that "none were involved in any kind of personal accountability group," and 100 percent of them had "ceased to invest in a personal time of prayer, Scripture reading, and worship."[5] It is impossible for us to continue to cling to even little sins and honestly interact with the presence of a righteous God. It doesn't make a whole lot of difference what Scripture passage we are reading. If we are nourishing sin in our lives, God will be nudging our hearts until we deal with that sin. It's the same with prayer. Just coming into the presence of God through these disciplines forces us to confront our sin. The only options left are to repent, confess, and eliminate the sin; to cease time with God in His Word and prayer; or, out of sheer discipline, to continue to read and pray in a state of hypocritical denial.

Church becomes a less-than-happy experience for us when we refuse to deal with sin in our lives. If we continue to go to church, we are tempted to deal with the righteous reminder by discounting the importance and impact of it through a critical attitude. Harboring sin in our lives makes it easy to focus on the hypocrites in church (we rarely include ourselves in the list), the music, the preaching, or a dozen other excuses for not letting the gathering of the saints and the proclamation of the Word of God be used of Him to motivate us to purity.

Godly people are particularly irritating to us when we cling to our sin. We love to find their flaws, gossip about their shortcomings, and tell ourselves that we would never really want to be *that* holy. After all, there's got to be more to life than just being sacred all the time.

These are the signals that we are well established in the far country. Before you absorb the rest of the chapter, use them as markers. Are any of them reflective of attitudes or activities in your life? What could you do to reverse the direction and turn your face toward home? Any sense of satisfaction in an intimate relationship with God requires that we deal with the drift.

We must also identify and deal with the obstructions.

THE OBSTRUCTED VIEW

There are only two really great baseball parks left in America: Fenway Park in Boston and Wrigley Field in Chicago. The other great old stadiums have been torn down and replaced with big, plasticized stadiums that lack character, charm, and closeness. The problem, however, with the old stadiums is that they have seats right behind posts. Those seats are called "seats with an obstructed view." If you have one of them, you can miss most of the action. You have to keep asking the person sitting next to you, "What happened?" You end up getting the game secondhand.

Many of us are in the park but in seats with an obstructed view. We hear the rejoicing, the praising, and the worship. We hear of the Spirit's work and of valiant feats in spiritual warfare. We hear of answered prayer and of love for one another—but it's all secondhand. We look down to the field boxes and say, "How did they get those seats? I wish I could be there. I want to be down close where I can be a firsthand participant." Before we learn how to get out of the cheap seats to where the action is, let's identify four pillars in the park that obstruct our view of the person of Christ.

1. The stuff of life

God warned the Israelites before they went into the Promised Land that the very things He was giving them could become substitutes for Him, causing them to forget how much they needed Him.

The *stuff* of life obstructs our view. It's being consumed with the gifts God has given to us and forgetting that He is the Giver. Affluence and abundance chill the fire of our hearts toward Jesus Christ. In the early days of America, when our nation was agrarian, the pioneers knew they needed God. They ate from the land. They needed the sun—but not too much of it. They needed the rain—but not too much of it. They needed the harvest in due season. They needed their flocks to be healthy in order to survive and thrive. They prayed to God to help them and to supply for them, and prayer drew them close to Him.

Today, if we get hungry we can go to a candy machine or run across the street to the grocery store. If we need something to wear, we don't have to shear the lambs (and trust they've been fed well enough) and sew our own clothes. We can go to the mall and flick out the plastic genie—you know, the one with the racing stripes.

I've always been fascinated by God's requiring Abraham to sacrifice his son. The requirement made absolutely no sense. God had already asked Abraham to move to a new land where He would give him a son. That son was to become the father of a great nation. Isaac embodied the heartbeat of what God had planned for Abraham. Yet now God was asking Abraham to put the young man on an altar and sacrifice him back to God.

With an amazing sense of obedience to God, Abraham obeyed. As Abraham lifted the trembling knife, God stopped him and provided a substitute sacrifice. God now knew that Abraham feared and valued Him more than anything he possessed. Abraham lived in a Canaanite civilization that practiced child sacrifice as its supreme expression of consecration to gods of wood and stone. Would Abraham be willing to love the true God with the dedication pagans felt toward their gods? He passed the test.

The test for us is to ask ourselves, *How loosely do I hold what God has supplied?* If this God to whom we are drawing close requires a dearly held commodity, would we give it up for Him? What is there in our lives that we possess that we would not give up for the ongoing joy of intimacy with Him? Are there things, persons, places, and habits we love more than we love Him? If so, we will always be in the cheap seats.

Intimacy is fanned where there is nothing more important to me than my deepening relationship with the one that I love.

It works this way in marriage.

It works this way with God.

2. Self

If *stuff* doesn't obstruct us, *self* probably will. If anyone had a right to be self-absorbed, it was the apostle Paul. I must admit that I'm impressed with his résumé. In Philippians 3:5–6 he lists his credentials: "Circumcised the eighth day" (that was exactly the way it was supposed to be; he was a good Jew), "of the nation of Israel, of the tribe of Benjamin" (that was the elite tribe), "a Hebrew of Hebrews; as to the Law, a Pharisee; as to zeal, a persecutor of the church; as to the righteousness which is in the Law, found blameless." Most of us would be preoccupied with our own importance if we carried his portfolio of accomplishments. Surprisingly, he wasn't. He goes on to say,

> But whatever things were gain to me, those things I have counted as loss for the sake of Christ. More than that, I count all things to be loss in view of the surpassing value of knowing Christ Jesus my Lord, for whom I have suffered the loss of all things, and count them but rubbish so that I may gain Christ, and may be found in Him, not having a righteousness of my own derived from the Law, but that which is through faith in Christ, the righteousness which comes from God on the basis of faith, that I may know Him and the power

of His resurrection and the fellowship of His sufferings, being conformed to His death (Philippians 3:7–10).

If we are consumed with self, we will not be consumed with Christ. We cannot have it both ways. Paul's choice was to forget the things of his past and to count all of his credentials as loss, that he might be free to pursue Christ.

In order to be born into a relationship with Christ, we have to come with empty hands. Salvation is not of our own works. The ground at the cross is level. We may come to the cross laden with accomplishments and acclaim, but in order to win Christ we must lay them down and cling, naked of credentials, to those old rugged timbers. And Paul makes clear that we must *continue* to count it all as loss, that we might know Him in a deeper, more intimate way.

We don't move to the field boxes by saying we hate self. Self-centeredness, selfishness, and turning self inward *are* bad, but self by itself is not. We can't ignore what Christ said to the Pharisees. He said that we should love the Lord our God with all of our *self* (Matthew 22:36–37). Self is intended to be a gift to God. But instead, we keep taking self back and putting it at the center where Christ belongs. It's no wonder we have difficulty seeing Him clearly. We need to ask Him to take it—to take all our heart, all our soul, all our mind, all our strength—all of self for Him. This is the joy of connectedness. This is a step toward intimacy.

3. Systems

If *stuff* or *self* doesn't get us, then the *systems* of a ritualized Christianity just might. All of us fight the tendency to subtly shift from a faith motivated by a growing personal relationship with Christ to a habitual, hollow life in a system that we've learned to conform to. We see this obstruction reflected in the church at Ephesus, to which Christ says,

To the angel of the church in Ephesus write: The One who holds the seven stars in His right hand, the One who walks among the seven golden lampstands, says this: "I know your deeds and your toil and perseverance, and that you cannot tolerate evil men, and you put to

the test those who call themselves apostles, and they are not, and you found them to be false; and you have perseverance and have endured for My name's sake, and have not grown weary" (Revelation 2:1–3).

At first blush we'd vote for the church at Ephesus to get the "Church of the Year" award. Christ showers it with bouquets of affirmation. But we read on. Christ says, "But I have this against you." That's an unsettling charge. We revel in the claim in Romans 8:31, "If God is for us, who is against us?" but what if the reverse is true? Christ states the charge: "You have left your first love" (Revelation 2:4). The Greek word for "first" here doesn't mean first in terms of time. It's not referring to how we felt the first day we got saved. Christ is not asking for that, because we'll never feel exactly that same way again until we get home. It means first in terms of priority or preeminence. Christ is saying that the Ephesians have abandoned Him as the priority of their love. They are busy doing all the right religious things, but they are not doing them because they love Him.

Why do we resist temptation? Because we might get caught or because there are consequences? Why do we give our money? So He will bless us in return? Why do we teach or serve on committees and boards? For our own glory? Because nobody else will do it? Do we sing in the choir because we love to sing? These are the marks of being busy for God within the system for wrong reasons. This is Christ's point. All we do should be about Him, for Him, and because of Him.

We need to cultivate a heart that resists temptation because we love Christ. We need to see saying no to sin as our opportunity to say to Him that we love Him more than that seemingly irresistible urge in our life. We give our money to His kingdom because it's one small way we can say we love Him, whether we will ever get anything back or not. It is for Him that we teach, preach, and sing. He must become the consuming, compelling reason—for all of life.

How do we get back down to the field boxes? We do so by obeying what Christ tells us. Repent and remember how it was at the beginning when we did the right things because we loved Christ more than anything else (Revelation 2:5). As we start reprioritizing Him in our lives, we will begin to do things because of who His is and as an expression of our love for Him.

When we refocus our activities on our love for Him, it is clearly a moment of reconnecting with Him. Doing what we do because of a relationship is a step toward intimacy.

4. Sin

If *stuff* doesn't obstruct our view, and if *self* and the *systems* of religion don't hinder us, then the *sin* in our lives surely will. We saw the dynamic clearly in Genesis 3. Adam and Eve sinned. God walked back into the garden, and what did they do? They hid. Our sin is so incompatible with a holy God that if we permit known sin to continue in our lives, we will always sit behind the post of our offense toward Him. In fact, we'll want to hide behind the poles so He won't notice us.

> If stuff *doesn't obstruct our view, and if* self *and the* systems *of religion don't hinder us, then the* sin *in our lives surely will.*

But God is still calling us from our isolation and aloneness. He is there, ready and waiting to cleanse and restore us. We need to keep short accounts with sin. If we are to draw near to God, we need to deal with sin immediately and completely.

In the process of recovery from sin, we may need to seek help from a Christian brother or sister. We may need a trusted friend, someone to pray for us, to be honest with us, and to hold us accountable for our recovery. Someone to keep us walking in purity.

I need to be around friends who are more mature in Christ than I. It motivates me to go farther with Christ and to walk more closely with Him. Find one or two. Walk with them; listen and learn from them. Just being around people who are close to Christ encourages us to decrease the distance.

When I was dating I always enjoyed the moment of anticipation when it came time to pick her up for that special evening together. I would drive to her house, walk up the sidewalk, and press the doorbell—and when she answered, we'd walk down the sidewalk together, and, being the gentleman that I am, I'd open the car door for her. She'd slide in and I'd shut the door. As I walked around the car to my door, I hoped that she was in the process of sliding over to be as close to me as possible. (Of course, this was back in those no-seatbelt, pre-bucket-seat days when all the cars had bench seats!) But I have to confess that sometimes, instead of sliding over, she'd be hugging the door. I knew something had happened between us, and job number one was to fix it.

I find myself wondering if that's how God feels about us. He's courted us, redeemed us, and made us His own. Yet to His disappointment He discovers that while we are content to *ride* with Him, there's a significant and increasing *distance* between us.

I love the hymn "Nothing Between" by Charles A. Tindley:

Nothing between my soul and the Savior,
Naught of this world's delusive dream;
I have renounced all sinful pleasure,
Jesus is mine; There's nothing between.

Nothing between, like worldly pleasure,
Habits of life though harmless they seem,
Must not my heart from Him e'er sever,
He is my all; There's nothing between.

Nothing between, like pride or station,
Self or friends shall not intervene,
Tho' it may cost me much tribulation,
I am resolved; There's nothing between.

Nothing between my soul and the Savior,
So that His blessed face may be seen;
Nothing preventing the least of His favor,
Keep the way clear! Let nothing between.

This is the song of the pilgrim who has left the far country to head for home.

A PRODIGAL'S PROGRESS

The Prodigal's life reflects the power of stuff, self, systems, and sin to set our lives in the wrong direction. His initial request was for his share of "stuff" from his father's estate. His commitment was to self as he left home. He didn't even pretend to have a religious system, yet he certainly set up a secular one to get him through life—a system that resulted in poverty, depression, loss of freedom, and personal shame. Eventually he realized that his main obstacle was the sin of insulting his father with his arrogance and self-promoting spirit of independence.

The Prodigal Son had to suffer the consequences of his self-centered life. First, he chose to hire himself out to some stranger as a means of support. Then, as a result, his new boss "sent him into his fields to feed swine" (Luke 15:15). This would be one of the most offensive jobs imaginable to a young man who had grown up in a good Jewish home, but the position he had put himself in didn't leave him much of a choice.

The Prodigal Son was humbled and ready to repent. "When he came to his senses, he said, 'How many of my father's hired men have more than enough bread, but I am dying here with hunger!'" (Luke 15:17). Home was where he knew he needed and wanted to be. The far country had betrayed him—as it always does. But he knew that he had to deal with the obstacles separating him from his father.

His solution?

"And the son said to him, 'Father, I have sinned against heaven and in your sight; I'm no longer worthy to be called your son'" (Luke 15:21).

Surprisingly, thankfully, the father forgave and restored the wanderer to full fellowship.

And so it is with our God. He is waiting, wanting, and wooing us to come home.

six

WHO'S THAT KNOCKING?

The Pursuit of a God Who Desires Intimacy

BEHOLD, THE TABERNACLE OF GOD IS AMONG MEN,
AND HE WILL DWELL AMONG THEM.
—REVELATION 21:3

I have to assume that at many colleges, one of the most exciting places on campus is the campus post office. As long as you have a clear conscience, the daily mail is a lot of fun. Students go looking for a letter from that special guy or girl at home. A check from Mom or Dad. A box of cookies. That grade on the last major test. I wonder what would happen if we were to pull a letter out of our stack of mail that had "Christ: The Universe" as the return address. While we would no doubt be concerned about what might be inside, knowing that He is well aware of all our shortcomings, we would be riveted to its text. We need to be riveted to the text of the letter Christ wrote to the church at Laodicea (Revelation 3:14–22). It is intensely personal and highly relevant to our search for intimacy. It could have been written to us. Near the end of the letter there is a compelling invitation:

> *Behold, I stand at the door and knock; if anyone hears My voice and opens the door, I will come in to him and will dine with him, and he with Me. He who overcomes, I will grant to him to sit down with Me on My throne, as I also overcame and sat down with My Father on His throne. He who has an ear, let him hear what the Spirit says to the churches (vv. 20–22).*

Although many times people have understood this passage to be about salvation, the context dictates that it's really about a relationship with Christ for those who have already come to know Him.

Christ is standing at the door of our hearts, knocking. The metaphor is powerful. It means that Christ is intentionally, aggressively, passionately pursing us. There are no qualifiers here. He isn't speaking just to the few really select, highly spiritual, worthy people at Laodicea. He is addressing *all* of the Laodiceans—the weak and the strong and the rich and the poor; those with disabilities and those who are marginalized. Christ portrays Himself as intentionally pursing intimacy with us.

All through Scripture God demonstrates His interest in intimacy. As we have noted, He walked back into the garden to find Adam and Eve and restore them to intimacy with Him. Throughout the whole history of Israel, God consistently pursued His people. Why would God want to live in the wilderness when He had heaven? He asked the Israelites to build a little portable house for Him because He wanted to be among them. And He kept satisfying them and sustaining them with manna and protecting them from great enemies. God was among His people.

> *The whole history of Scripture explodes with the fact that God is busy about intentionally pursuing intimacy with us.*

And then, in a greatly anticipated event, like birth pangs in Israel, the Messiah was born. God came in the flesh. In the Greek text of John 1:14, the apostle graphically says that Christ "pitched His tent among us." He touched those of us who were lame and made us walk. He made those of us who were blind to see. He called His friend Lazarus to come forth from the dead. He said to His disciples, "Follow Me." And when He left He told them, "I go to prepare a place for you. If I go, . . . I will come again and receive you to Myself, that where I am, there you may be also" (John 14:2–3). The whole history of Scripture explodes with the fact that God is busy about intentionally pursuing intimacy with us.

Scripture begins with God's pursuing Adam and Eve in the garden to repair their shattered relationship and restore them to fellowship with Him, and it ends with His finishing the task and locking us into permanent, unthreatened intimacy. John records it for us:

> *Then I saw a new heaven and a new earth; for the first heaven and the first earth passed away, and there is no longer any sea. And I saw the holy city,new Jerusalem, coming down out of heaven from God, made ready as a bride adorned for her husband. And I heard a loud voice from the throne, saying, "Behold, the tabernacle of God is among men, and He will dwell among them, and they shall be His people, and God Himself will be among them, and He will wipe away every tear from their eyes; and there will no longer be any death; there will no longer be any mourning, or crying, or pain; the first things have passed away (Revelation 21:1–4).*

If Christ makes Himself so accessible, why is it that we don't open the door? There are at least three reasons for our reticent response.

FEAR

Though God does pursue us and though Christ is there knocking, some of us may be afraid to open the door. Many of us have longed for intimacy in human relationships—with our father, or mother, or someone else—only to find that our hopes for intimacy were not only dashed and broken but that as we made ourselves vulnerable, we were wounded in the process. We are afraid. We just don't know if we can ever trust again.

In *Intimacy with God*, Thomas Keating speaks to the problem:

The Christian's spiritual path is based on a deepening trust in God. It is trust that first allows us to take that initial leap in the dark, to encounter God at deeper levels of ourselves. And it is trust that guides the intimate refashioning of our being, the transformation of our pain, woundedness, and unconscious motivation into the person that God intended us to be. Because trust is so important, our spiritual journey may be blocked if we carry negative attitudes toward God from early childhood. If we are afraid of God or see God as an angry father-figure, a suspicious policeman, or a harsh judge, it will be hard to develop enthusiasm, or even an interest in the journey.[1]

I have a prayer for those of us who keep God far away, who hear the knocking but fear to risk opening the door. It is the prayer of Mark 9:24: "Lord, I believe; help thou mine unbelief!" (KJV). We need to pray, "Lord I *want* to trust You," and then move toward trusting Him and being venturesome enough to reach out and open the door to God. We need to grasp the truth that God will not disappoint us. He will not abuse us. He will not use us. He died for us—He already proved how much He cares for us. No one who has trusted God and moved toward intimacy has ultimately been disappointed—ever.

SELF-SUFFICIENCY

But for some of us, the fact that Christ is still on the outside may have something to do with the problem of the Christians at Laodicea. Revelation 3:20–22 tells the story of many of our lives.

To the angel of the church in Laodicea write:

The Amen, the faithful and true Witness, the Beginning of the creation of God, says this:

"I know your deeds, that you are neither cold nor hot; I wish that you were cold or hot. So because you are lukewarm, and neither hot nor cold, I will spit you out of My mouth. Because you say, 'I am rich, and have become wealthy, and have need of nothing,' and you do not know that you are wretched and miserable and poor and blind and naked, I advise you to buy from Me gold refined by fire so that you may become rich, and white garments so that you may clothe yourself, and that the shame of your nakedness will not be revealed; and eye salve to anoint your eyes so that you may see. Those whom I love, I reprove and discipline; therefore be zealous and repent" (vv. 14–19).

In effect, Christ says to the Laodiceans, "You are lukewarm. I wish you were like iced tea on a hot day or like hot tea on a cold day. I just wish you had an edge on you, but because you are neither hot nor cold you are distasteful to me."

Why would God say that about His people? He said it because of their sense of self-sufficiency. They were rich and had no material needs, so they thought they didn't need God. They relied on what they consumed materially in order to satisfy, sustain, and secure themselves.

I find it interesting that all these "self" terms we throw around the church make us wilt with instant guilt. Just say the word *self-centered* and we wince. Self-indulgent . . . Self-serving. But when we think of self-sufficiency, our eyes glaze over with pious apathy. We don't think it's as bad as the other "self" words. But it's a big issue to God. Christ said of the Laodiceans that though they had all the "stuff"—comforts, companions, and commodities—they were "wretched and miserable and poor and blind and naked" (v. 17). They needed Christ.

But Christ didn't give up on the Laodiceans, just like He doesn't give up on us. In 1 Timothy 6 Paul tells believers to stop fleeing after earthly riches and to "Pursue righteousness, godliness, faith, love, perseverance and gentleness" (v. 11). God wants to make us rich in the right ways. He wants to fill our lives with truly valuable treasures. He wants to give us "gold refined by fire" (Revelation 3:18). He wants us to have His peace, comfort, presence, and power. He wants to make us rich in a relationship that has access to all His resources. He wants to clothe our nakedness with white robes, the

> *Until we learn to be content with what we have, we may never know how wonderfully content we can be in Him.*

gowns of His children, and to anoint our eyes with the salve of His presence so that we can see (v. 18). And, as He told the Laodiceans, He wants us to repent of our self-sufficiency (v. 19). It's all because He loves us.

I love the fact that Christ unrelentingly pursues intimacy with us. We should feel ashamed of the fact that through so much of our Christian life we have assumed that it was to institutions that we should be committed. That His gifts and His goodness and the affluence and the abundance and the friends and the context of my Christianity were all I really needed. The sin of my self-sufficiency is an offense of the deepest kind to Him. Yet He still knocks.

Unfortunately, we are so busy scrambling to find more of this world's goods to satisfy ourselves that we hardly know He is there. Until we learn to be content with what we have, we may never know how wonderfully content we can be in Him.

DISCONTENT

Laurence Shames, in his penetrating analysis of Americans' preoccupation with consumption, *The Hunger for More,* writes:

> More. If there's a single word that summarizes American hopes and obsessions, that's it. More money. More success. More luxuries and gizmos. We live for more—for our next raise, our next house; and the things we already have, however wonderful they are, tend to pale in comparison with the things we might still get.[2]

A friend who is an heiress to a massive estate told me that she wished she could have the days back again when getting a mug for Christmas would please and satisfy her. She remarked that there was a certain wonder and pleasure to find joy and satisfaction in small things.

What she had forgotten was that even those of us who *can* find pleasure in a new mug soon find that it too becomes commonplace. There is that ever-present craving for all that is more, bigger, or better.

I love heavy, large porcelain mugs. It's probably a male thing. My all-time favorite is my Chicago Bulls mug. That is it *was*, until I visited the Hot Shot Café in Asheville, North Carolina. You have to experience the Hot Shot Café to appreciate what a privilege it is. It's where the local of the locals hangs out. Old jukebox and all. No pretense. Just good ol' home cookin' and an authentically rude waitress. On the shelf behind the cash register were Hot Shot Café mugs. I knew I needed one. It was a compulsion I couldn't resist. So I left some of my hard-earned cash behind and took my prized mug home where it would take its place among the other mugs I have bought through the years to satisfy my longings.

If it were only the mugs in our lives—or the teddy bears, or CDs, or antiques, or cars—it wouldn't really be all that big a deal. But it's the dynamic that drives my need for just one more mug that drives the bigger issues of life as well.

Shames goes on to say,

> During the past decade, many people came to believe there didn't have to be a purpose. The mechanism didn't require it. Consumption kept the workers working, which kept the paychecks coming, which kept the people spending, which kept inventors inventing and investors investing, which meant there was more to consume. The system, properly understood, was independent of values and needed no philosophy to prop it up. It was a perfect circle, complete in itself—and empty in the middle.[3]

The biblical word for satisfaction is the word *contentment*. We are called to be content with what we have since we have God—and He is fully sufficient. That doesn't mean we don't ever want something or that we don't enjoy a purchase

> *We are called to be content with what we have since we have God—and He is fully sufficient.*

here and there. It means that we are not controlled by passions to consume. Having Him, we have it all. Anything extra is a bonus. Paul testified that he had learned both how to have plenty and how to have little and in both cases to be content (Philippians 4:11–13). In 1 Timothy 6 he writes,

> *But godliness actually is a means of great gain when accompanied by contentment. For we have brought nothing into the world, so we cannot take anything out of it either. If we have food and covering, with these we shall be content. But those who want to get rich fall into temptation and a snare and many foolish and harmful desires that plunge men into ruin and destruction. For the love of money is*

the root of all sorts of evil, and some by longing for it have wan-dered away from the faith and pierced themselves with many griefs (vv. 6–10).

The King James Version puts verse 6 this way: "Godliness with con-tentment is great gain." We often reverse the formula to say "godliness plus gain is contentment" when in reality godliness plus contentment equals gain. The writer to the Hebrews reminds us,

Make sure that your character is free from the love of money, being content with what you have; for He Himself has said, "I will never desert you, nor will I ever forsake you," so that we confidently say, "The Lord is my helper, I will not be afraid. What will man do to me?" (13:5–6).

Contentment is not just reflected in our relationship to things. We can be discontented with our spouse, our job, our place in life, our edu-cation, or a long list of other things. Sometimes discontentment can motivate us to righteousness or a more zealous commitment to God. This is a healthy kind of discontentment. The kind of discontentment, however, that signals a vulnerability to aloneness is a discontentment that seeks personal satisfaction and security in "just one more thing, one more experience, one more friendship."

There is no way that we will want to turn our backs to the far coun-try and our faces toward home until we are ready to realize that Christ is our all-sufficient source and as such enables us to live in the calm peace of a contented life.

When He is knocking, it is a trusting, God-sufficient, contented heart that hurries to answer. Opening the door generates the pleasure of experiencing His promise: "I will come in to him and will dine with him, and he with Me" (Revelation 3:20).

PRODIGAL'S PROGRESS

When we last saw the Prodigal Son, he had decided to go back to his father—even if it meant becoming one of his servants. He had been far from home too long. He wanted to restore that sense of closeness, regardless of the cost.

The turning point in the life of the Prodigal Son occurred when he changed his perspective on life on his own. With a big chunk of his father's inheritance in hand, he had expected the rest of his life to run smoothly. He had expected lots of friends and popularity. He expected the best. And while he was able to enjoy those things temporarily, they were no substitute for life with his father. He finally "came to his senses" and realized what a faithful provider and good person his father really was. And he longed for home.

As the story continues, we discover *how* his expectations are changing. "I will get up and go to my father, and will say to him, 'Father, I have sinned against heaven, and in your sight; I am no longer worthy to be called your son; make me as one of your hired men'" (Luke 15:18–19). His thoughts are now focused less on his material rights and privileges than on the relationship. He finally realizes that if he doesn't have the relationship, he has nothing.

> As soon as the son was ready, the father was readily accessible.

We've all been in situations where we decide to reach out to someone and try to restore a relationship. We're never quite sure how the other person will respond, so our stomachs are usually in knots and our hearts racing. Perhaps that's how the Prodigal Son felt each step closer to home.

If so, it was wasted anxiety. The narrative continues: "So he got up and came to his father. But while he was still a long way off, his father saw him and felt compassion for him, and ran and embraced him and kissed him" (Luke 15:20).

Did the father just happen to notice him a long way off? Or was he keeping a vigil? Did he keep his eyes to the horizon, waiting and hoping for the day his wayward son would find his way home again? I think so. The son was an object of his father's love and was no doubt stunned by his father's grace and mercy. There was no probation. No lectures. Just a celebration.

As soon as the son was ready, the father was readily accessible. So it is for us as well. The very second we decide to get up and answer the door, we find that God is there, ready to come in. It's a union that our souls will never forget.

seven

REPENTANT RELIANCE

New Directions

THEN MEN BEGAN TO CALL UPON THE
NAME OF THE LORD.
—GENESIS 4:26

Everyone wants to be needed. It's intrinsically tied to our sense of worth and value. If my wife, Martie, didn't need me and Harvest Bible Chapel didn't need me and my children didn't need me, my life would lose much of its purpose and drive. In fact, all of our significant relationships rotate on the axis of needing and being needed. When we lose sight of the fact that people need us and we need them, intimacy in special relationships begins to fade.

While all of us want to be needed and want to relate to someone whom we need, there is no relationship in which this becomes more crucial than our personal relationship with Jesus Christ. We need Him. There is no one more deserving to be the focus of our dependence and the absolute, all-sufficient resource for everything in life than Jesus Christ. That's why it's so strange that He would be standing outside the door of our lives knocking to come in.

Intimacy demands that we repent. Coming home involves an intentional commitment to transition from a life that finds its sufficiency in the shallow goods and quick-hit experiences this world has to offer to a life that focuses on the person of Jesus Christ. In fact, that's exactly what Revelation 3:19 urges—no, *commands*—us to do. Christ prefaces His knocking by stating, "Those whom I love, I reprove and discipline; therefore be zealous and repent."

The process of intimacy rises and falls on our understanding and actualizing the concept of repentance. This concept is most often characterized in the New Testament by the Greek word *metanoēo*. The root of its meaning and the base of its applications is the reality that repentance means changing our minds about a particular pattern of behavior and, as a result of that change of mind, turning our lives in the opposite direction toward new patterns of action and reaction. It means not only changing our minds about what is right and what we ought to do but also changing our minds completely about what we have done in the past. As the *New International Dictionary of New Testament Theology* says, "Whenever someone gives his thought and life a new direction, it always involves a judgment on his previous views and behaviour."[1]

> *The process of intimacy rises and falls on our understanding and actualizing the concept of repentance.*

WHAT DOES IT MEAN TO REPENT?

Given that intimacy rises and falls on repentance, what does it mean to change our minds about our past behavior and turn our lives around toward new behavior? First, the particular grammatical configuration of the Greek in Revelation 3:20 is striking. It's called an "aorist imperative." In this verse it means that repentance from the wretched self-sufficiency that drove us from the face of God and left us alone is an action that takes place at a particular point in our lives and marks the beginning of a whole new track for us.

What is interesting is that, as Nigel Turner notes in his *Grammar of New Testament Greek*, "the selection of the aorist imperative, in contrast to the present imperative, is a more pressing, actually rude and ruthless, statement."[2] In this sense, God "gets in our face" about this matter. The aorist imperative here has the effect of slamming us against a wall. God is stopping us in our tracks, which gives us cause to change our minds about our direction of life and turn to a better way. It is about knowing that the energy of aloneness lurks beneath the surface of our souls, is about knowing how offensive our self-sufficiency has been, and is about being ready to come home. In terms of the process of intimacy, that better way is turning toward Christ as the center of our souls, the ultimate and only reliable source for satisfaction, sustenance, and security.

STEPS IN REPENTANCE

Turning our backs on the aloneness of the far country, repenting of our self-sufficiency, and starting toward home involves four distinct steps.

Step 1: We need to clearly judge past patterns that have kept us in a far country.

This means that we need to deal dramatically with our rationalizations and excuses. We must admit to ourselves and to others that we have been wrong to think the way we have about our self-satisfied, self-sustained lives. We must make this admission without qualification or excuse.

I'm reminded of the clear, compelling way Paul described his change from self-serving ways to a totally Christ-reliant existence. In Galatians 2:20 he says, "I am crucified with Christ" (KJV). We have tended to romanticize the cross. In our culture we miss how graphically crucifixion portrayed the finality of dealing with sins. It dealt with criminal behavior in the most brutal fashion. No citizen of Rome would ever be judged on a cross. Rather, this ancient instrument of torture was a place for finally and fully dealing with foreigners, aliens, and strangers who had committed criminal acts.

Crosses were not raised high, as we often see in pictures; rather, the feet of the one being crucified were usually no more than two feet off the ground so that people could look into the eyes of the condemned and express their scorn in words that showed how much they despised the offender and his behavior. The custom was that the offender would not be taken off the cross until his legs were broken, to be sure that the job was complete.

Not only have we romanticized the cross, we have romanticized the death of Christ. We have rightly said that Christ died on the cross as

One who didn't deserve to die. And while that is true, we *did* deserve to die, and He bore the criminal acts of our lives in His body on the tree. In that sense the cross was a just and necessary experience.

For Paul, repentance meant that he viewed the totality of his life as a criminal act, and, with brutal finality, he himself was nailed with Christ to the cross. You and I won't know real intimacy with Christ until we take the list of sins in our lives that separate us from Christ—and the list of the self-serving, self-sufficient attitudes in our lives, plus the attitude of being content to lean and depend on everything but Christ—and nail them with brutal finality to the cross with Him. We need to stand before our sins and look them in the eye and despise them as the criminals who have wrought havoc on our souls and debilitated our capacity to come home from the far country to meet Christ in the depths of our souls. This is true repentance.

Step 2: Since we are never perfect, we need to be progressively pursuing repentance.

This means that we should live in a continuing state of repentance.

By this I don't mean that we can go back to visit past failures with sorrow and shame afresh. That would only be self-defeating and unnecessary. Our sins were dealt with two thousand years ago when Christ bore those criminal acts in Himself. When we are tempted to go back and feel the sorrow and shame, we should resist the urge and use the moment as a springboard for gratitude toward God for the wonderful deliverance He has given to us from those things.

Progressive repentance is living our lives every day in a state of open honesty, seeing ourselves as we really are and then immediately taking the criminal elements of our lives that distance our souls from Christ and nailing them to the cross.

I have found it to be cleansing and liberating to look every day for new areas of my life that I can nail to the cross in repentance. As I have been committed to this kind of daily vulnerability, God has been quick to show me new ways in which I can remove the obstructions between us.

Early on in my ministry when I had a lot more time to enjoy leisure activities, I used to occupy the open spaces in my calendar by refinishing antique furniture. It started out not as a hobby but as a necessity, as Martie and I would scarf through antique shops and used furniture stores to find things we liked that would have value if we fixed them up.

Refinishing antique furniture is a rewarding experience––not the hard work of the process but the beauty of the product. Actually the process is long and difficult. You start by using strong chemicals that can peel your skin or get you high, or both, and strip off the old varnish and residue of wax that has accumulated over the years. Once that is done, the next step is to take heavy-grade sandpaper and sand the daylights out of the piece of furniture. What is important is not just the highly exposed areas but also the crooks and crannies of the piece, where the repair and restoration of the fine detail gives it its finished beauty. After using the coarse sandpaper, you then take increasingly less coarse sandpaper and repeat the sequence until you finally have a smooth finish. At that point you apply the first coat of varnish. When the varnish dries, you're still not through. Now comes the fine sandpaper that rubs nearly all the varnish off. Then another coat. Then sanding again with finer grades of paper. At that point it's time for more coats of varnish and more rubbing. Then it's time to use steel wool––until you have a finish as smooth as the windshield of your car. At that point you apply another coat of varnish, only to rub it off again, and then still *another* coat, which you rub down once more until you finally have a product that is fit to display the glory of its original intended beauty.

Refinishing good furniture reflects what God wants to do with us throughout our whole experience with Him. The first steps are the most brutal. The cutting of the chemical stripper to purify our souls from obvious and flagrant sin is often painful and the process radical. But that's not the end of it. It's continuing to sand, varnish, use steel wool, varnish, and rub—until step by step, layer by layer, our lives begin to reflect the brilliant sheen of the glory of Jesus Christ.

That is the nature of progressive repentance. And that is what Paul meant when he said that, having nailed all the criminal elements of his life to the cross with Christ, he was now dead. But not *really* dead, for the risen Christ now lived through his life.

Those who wish to deepen their intimacy with Christ do not wait for the impact of a reproof or an emotional confrontation or the fear of consequences to bring them up short about their sins. They live in a mode of being willing, ready, and waiting to repent, until God rubs out the smallest and almost imperceptible blemishes we would hardly notice if we weren't striving to have the purity of Christ living through us.

Step 3: Develop a heart and mind that welcomes God's reproofs.

Sometimes God needs to use reproofs to catch our attention. As Revelation 3:19 says, "Those whom I love, I reprove and discipline." As long as God loves us—which is all the way to eternity—He will reprove and discipline us to nudge and nurture us toward unhindered fellowship with Him. In order to be open to those reproofs, we must reject our normal defensive responses. We must scrap excuses and comparisons to others and resist the temptation to see ourselves as victims rather than responsible managers of our own existence.

If we've learned to be progressive repenters, we keep our hearts tuned to the voice of God, even when it is still and small.

As we have discussed in earlier sections of this book, reproofs come through those who are close to us, such as family and friends, or through other external circumstances such as consequences of sin. God reproves us internally through the work of the Holy Spirit and the impact of His Word within our hearts. If we've learned to be progressive repenters, we keep our hearts tuned to the voice of God, even when it is still and small.

We will welcome His reproof and instruction.

Step 4: Make purity a primary life goal.

Coming to grips with even the shallowest sense of the holiness of God makes us aware that He is in His character, conduct, and composure totally distinct from us as fallen individuals. While nothing short of the finished work of Jesus Christ on the cross gives us the privilege of standing in the presence of a holy God, purity on the practical level is what opens the door for us to access an unhindered experience with His presence.

Although we often think of purity in terms of moral behavior, we must remember that it is important to keep our motives pure as well. Pure motives begin with doing all that we do because we love Christ. It means doing all that we do for Him and ultimately for the glory of His name.

There is also purity of speech—choosing, framing, and forming our words to speak what is true and pure and right (Proverbs 25:11; Colossians 4:6).

There is the purity of our thought life (Philippians 4:8).

There is the purity of our pursuits (1 Timothy 6:6–11).

There is the purity of our passions (Psalm 42:1–2).

In the Beatitudes Christ powerfully links purity and intimacy. He taught, "Blessed are the pure in heart, for they shall see God (Matthew 5:8). The word *see* literally means "to continually see." It is a present reality. The purity that is forged in our hearts by a continuing spirit of repentance eliminates the haze and the smudge that hinder a close view of God.

These are the four steps of a repentant heart that enable us to turn our faces toward Christ without shame or hypocrisy. A life lived in a mode of repentance finds its heart resonating with the psalmist who said, "As for me, I said, 'O LORD, be gracious to me; heal my soul, for I have sinned against You'" (Psalm 41:4).

I am struck with the conclusion of Psalm 139, where David, in an unusual moment of vulnerability, invites the Lord to perform an ongoing spiritual EKG on the innermost parts of his being. He welcomes God with these words:

Search me, O God, and know my heart;
Try me and know my anxious thoughts;
And see if there be any hurtful way in me (vv. 23–24a).

Although those words probably have become numbingly familiar to most of us, they must be the words of our hearts if our souls are to bask in the satisfying reality of a close relationship with Jesus Christ. What I find most interesting about the psalmist's invitation to this core inspection is that after he repentantly opens himself up, he then makes a commitment to a new direction in life—to a radical sense of reliance upon God. He says, "And lead me in the everlasting way" (v. 24b).

DRAMATIC DEPENDENCE

As we have noted, it is the often undealt-with problem of self-reliance that keeps Christ standing on the outside knocking to come in. The Laodiceans thought they had need of nothing because they had everything. But as Christ so graphically tells them, though they think they are rich, they are really wretched, miserable, poor, blind, and naked (Revelation 3:17). It is at this point of frontal reproof that Christ offers them an invitation as the antidote to the vacancy of soul they are experiencing. He invites them to leave their preoccupation with consumerism and turn to Him. Since they are obsessed with the veiled bankruptcy of their own gain, He speaks to them in the language of merchandising. "I advise you to *buy* from Me" (v. 18, emphasis added). He asks them to come to Him just as they would come to a store for everything they need.

The first thing He offers in the marketplace of His provisions is "gold refined by fire" (v. 18). In those days gold was the ultimate wealth by which you could secure whatever you wanted and needed. Christ says that He offers the ultimate resource for all we need and want. In fact, He says that if we have the pure gold He offers, we will become truly rich.

No doubt the wealthy Laodiceans were lost in the intrigue of high fashion and trying to outsmart and outdress each other at the big social events of the year. So Jesus invites them to buy from Him "white garments so that you may clothe yourself, and that the shame of your nakedness will not be revealed" (v. 18). Christ purified these white garments by His finished work on the cross. What Christ is offering here is the prosperity of Himself and the pleasure of His purity.

Then He tells them He will sell them eye salve so that they might truly see (v. 18). This is no doubt a reference to the fact that when we fully rely on Jesus Christ, He enables us to see with discernment and accuracy so that we can judge correctly in all that we do and pursue.

Before we enumerate the steps we can take to develop this sense of radical reliance on Christ, let's reflect once more on the tragic history of Cain, in which all society plummeted to the depths of treachery and despair. We left Cain and those who followed him hopelessly separated from God and alone. Thankfully, by the end of Genesis 4, something new was emerging on the horizon as men were beginning to move from the savage despair of self-reliance (Genesis 4:23–24) to an uncompromising reliance on God.

> *When we fully rely on Jesus Christ, He enables us to see with discernment and accuracy so that we can judge correctly in all that we do and pursue.*

We learn that another child is born to Adam and Eve. He is named Seth because, as Eve put it, "God has appointed me another offspring in place of Abel, for Cain killed him" (v. 25). The Bible then goes on to say that Seth had a son, and he was named Enosh. Here a radical shift occurs in the account of the early downward spiral of humanity. It is a shift all of us must make if we are to know freedom from the grip of aloneness and its consequences. This strategic U-turn begins with the conviction that we need God, that a life functionally disconnected from Him is a life headed in the wrong direction. The text says that his name was called Enosh because his birth marked a shift away from self-reliance to a reliance on God. As the text says, "Then men began to call upon the name of the LORD" (v. 26).

To "call on the name of the LORD" literally means to recognize our dependence on Him. It is a confession of dependency. Calling on the name of the Lord is a shift from self-sufficiency to God-sufficiency; from independence to dependence; from life on my own terms to life on His terms; from isolation to intimacy.

This is where intimacy always begins. After repentance, dependence is the next step in drawing near to God.

It should not go unnoticed that before God's people were known as Hebrews or Christians, they were known as "the people who call on the name of the Lord." This is the heartbeat of our relationship to Him.

Cultivating this kind of mindset begins with an accurate view of ourselves. The assumption of dependence is that I am frail when left alone and that I need something beyond myself upon which I can fully and confidently depend. It is the persistent conviction that I need God.

Interestingly, the name *Enosh* literally means "the frail one." H. C. Leupold in his exposition of Genesis writes:

> We strongly cast our vote for this meaning: 'enôsh = the "frail one," "the mortal." Seth was so impressed with the weakness of mortals that he gave his son a name indicative of this truth. Such a name, however, does not reflect pessimism or discouragement. It is expressive of truth, deep, unvarnished truth. But the very next statement now goes on to show what this family did when their own frailty became clearly apparent to them: they turned all the more eagerly to their God and sought him, making a regular and public practice of it in worship.[3]

C. F. Keil and F. Delitzsch underscore the significance of this when they write: "To be weak, faint, frail, designates man from his frail and mortal condition . . . In this name, therefore, the feeling and knowledge of human weakness and frailty were expressed (the opposite of the pride and arrogance displayed by the Canaanitish family), and this feeling led to God."[4]

Girdlestone adds, "From the earliest days, the Name of Jehovah was taken as the embodiment of that hope for the human race which found its expression in sacrifice and in prayer."[5] Intimacy begins with a step of radical reliance that demonstrates itself in worship and submission.

So much works against this step. It requires a shift from pride to humility. We have to get beyond worldly position, gifts, prosperity, personal capacities, and skills to see that we need Him. All of the best that we have apart from God is only a charade, a mask that hides our real need. Conversely, when we yield all that we have to God, it becomes a resource of unlimited capacity for good and gain.

The worst deceit in all of life is the thought that we are not frail—that we are capable and crafty enough to go it on our own. The song by Annie S. Hawkes says it best:

I need Thee, O I need Thee;
Every hour I need Thee;
O bless me now, my Savior,
I come to Thee.

J. R. MacDuff, in his little book *Morning and Night Watches*, prays,

I come in the nothingness of the creature, exulting alone in the fullness of Jesus. I come, "just as I am without one plea," to Thee Almighty Savior. I seek to disown every creature confidence, and, with all the burden of my guilt, to cast myself for time and eternity at Thy feet . . . I cannot stand in myself . . . I have no other confidence and I need no other. Jesus, I am complete in Thee. Let me not look inwardly on myself, where there is everything to sink me in despondency and dismay; but let me look with the undivided and unwavering eye of faith to Thy bleeding sacrifice . . . And while with childlike faith I rest on the finished work of Jesus, may I have the same simple trust and confidence in all His dealings towards me. May I feel that the Shepherd of Israel cannot lead me wrong, that His own way must be the safest and the best. Lord, guide me with Thy counsel while I live. Take me—lead me—use me, as Thou seest good.[6]

It is this kind of reliance that starts us toward intimacy with God. As James wrote, we must first draw near to God if we expect Him to draw near to us (4:8). Holding Him at arm's length in our self-confidence only leads us farther from Him.

Who is that knocking at your door? Repent. Rely. Take the risk. Reach out. And He will come in. And when He comes in, know that He comes in to connect with us. "I will come in . . . and . . . dine" (Revelation 3:20). In the culture of the New Testament, dining together was the way intimacy in friendships was developed. That's why the Pharisees

Transitioning from a passive Christianity to an active intimacy requires ongoing repentance and a commitment to radical reliance.

were so put out when Christ was invited to attend and, worse yet, accepted invitations to eat with the worst kind of people in their world. The Pharisees express their disdain for Christ's behavior in Luke 15:2, where they angrily complain that Christ not only hangs out with sinners but "eats with them." When Christ offers to come in and dine with us, it is an offer of access to Him in an intimate friendship. He wants to come in and connect with us.

Connecting is not random. We don't just connect when and where we feel like it. As we will see, there are specific points at which we develop a deepening, connected friendship with the person of Jesus Christ.

Nor is it passive. Christ takes the initiative as He knocks on our door. We take the initiative to open up and welcome Him to the fellowship of our hearts. There isn't a relationship in the world that has been highly successful when one person has taken all the initiative and the other has been passive. I've found in nearly forty years of marriage that when I am really checked out of the relationship, something bad usually happens. I'd like to have a five-dollar bill for every time Martie has said, "Joe, have you listened to anything that I've said?" While she had been attempting to connect with me, I was off in church world or golf world or appointment world. I am in the greatest jeopardy when she has waxed eloquent through paragraphs of soul-revealing perspectives only to conclude with the question, "What do *you* think about that?" It's her way of welcoming my opinion. If I haven't been listening, I'm in the ditch! I usually try to rescue myself with the response, "Well, it's interesting. What do you think about it?" It rarely works.

Transitioning from a passive Christianity to an active intimacy requires ongoing repentance and a commitment to radical reliance.

A PRODIGAL'S PROGRESS

The return of the Prodigal was a dramatically wonderful event for both father and son. The father couldn't hide his feelings. His love came pouring out in embraces and kisses. And the son had worked through the steps we've just examined in this chapter:

- He left behind the thought and behavior patterns that had lured him far from home to begin with.
- He was truly repentant.
- He was sensitive to the reproofs of life.
- He was committed to purity from this point on.

The son's sincerity and humility are evident:

The son said to him, "Father, I have sinned against heaven, and in your sight; I am no longer worthy to be called your son."

But the father said to his slaves, "Quickly bring out the best robe and put it on him, and put a ring on his hand and sandals on his feet; and bring the fattened calf, kill it, and let us eat and celebrate; for this son of mine was dead and has come to life again; he was lost and has been found." And they began to celebrate (Luke 15:21–24).

The stage is set for intimacy. Rejoicing. A new beginning.

eight

CONNECTEDNESS

Drawing Close to God

To declare Your lovingkindness in the morning
And Your faithfulness by night.
Psalm 92:2

I have to confess that I am technically challenged.

Several years ago when we moved into a new home, I bought a whole new stereo system. I love music—I love it loud, I love it soft, and I love it big. I love it all the way across the continuum—jazz, blues, light rock, country, pop, and classical, depending on the mood I'm in. I love it all. So we bought a stereo with all the sophisticated nuances of volume, balance, and tone. Excitedly, I brought the boxes home and unwrapped the pieces of digitized equipment. There they were—wires and everything—and halfway into the project I was in the prenatal position, curled up under the kneehole of my desk, weeping, with cords tangled around my body! I just don't get technical stuff.

I think we're a lot like that in a spiritual sense. God has created, redeemed, and given us all we need for an intimate relationship with Him. And though we have all the equipment we need to connect to all the beauty and harmony of His glory to be pumped through us, we never quite seem to get it figured out. Spiritually, we are connectedly challenged.

Intimacy with God requires that we connect with Christ. This "plugging in" has a pattern and a sequence to it. Having all the wires is not enough. Applying them correctly in all the right places is what makes it work.

CONNECTING THROUGH PRAYER
AND THE WORD

How do we connect? I can hear you thinking, *Here we go again—I'll bet he's going to talk about reading the Bible and prayer!* You guessed it—it's at the top of my list. How else do we think we will connect intimately with God unless we are in a pattern of ongoing communication with Him?

It's like the old story of the woman who dragged her husband to the counselor and complained that he never said he loved her. To which the surprised husband turned to his wife and said, "Hey, when we got married I told you that I loved you, and if that ever changes, I'll let you know."

Marriages don't ever make it all the way to intimacy without ongoing loving communication. And Christians don't make it to intimacy with God unless they have established regular patterns of communication with Him.

Christians don't make it to intimacy with God unless they have established regular patterns of communication with Him.

Martie and I have been at the marriage thing for lots of years. Our lives and ministry have been busy and often distracted by events, emergencies, and the press and stress of ministerial responsibilities. My work for the Lord often takes me away from home. Martie and I have discovered that when we are away from each other, it is easy to create a distancing type of independence. We tend to develop our own systems of survival and schedule. And if the absence has been long enough, when we come together again there is a time of adjustment that can create tension. This was particularly true when our children were young. When I was gone, Martie was in charge of the kingdom. Everybody got used to the setup. And then I'd come home! In fact, I would come home thinking that everything was the way it had always been and that the scenery would adjust to revolve around me—in my dreams!

That is not unlike our relationship to God. When it comes to intimacy with Him, absence does not make the heart grow fonder. It makes it grow more distant. Seasons of absence from communing with God in prayer and through His Word make sin and self-sufficiency stronger and reentry difficult and challenging. Not only do we get out of practice, but also, having been apart from divine input, we develop systems of independence and patterns of thought and behavior that are immediately challenged by reentry. Intimacy requires a steady pouring out of our hearts in praise to God and prayer and the steady absorbing of His Word into our hearts.

Reading, meditating on, and studying the Bible is critical to connectedness. When is the best time to be in God's Word? For some, it is in the morning. My friend Ravi Zacharias, gifted evangelist and apologist, notes:

My wife and I for years have had a habit of going out every Sunday morning and enjoying a breakfast together. Recently I said to her, "A lot has happened in my life in the last few months that I am so grateful to God for; one of the most significant being the recovery of the early morning hours with God." I know that not everybody likes the early morning hours, and I don't like them either. But let me be candid; the surge of emotion is going to storm you every day, possibly with some disappointment, some hurt, some heartbreak, some conflict, some argument, and probably, some struggle. The best way I know how to face each day is to prepare the heart first thing in the morning before the pace picks up, to let God speak to your heart before you do anything else. When I study in the morning (I say this with God as my witness), that next one and a half to two hours are the hours I enjoy the most every day. I have paced the floor. I have read His Word. I have drawn closer to my Lord, and I have come to the conclusion after all of the years that I have been a believer, that the best days are the days where I've heard from Him first. "Early will I seek thee," says the psalmist. My dear friend, if you ever want to know the victory over feelings, try this: Go early and seek Him so that He prepares that heart of yours. If you don't do that, the emotions will knock you over by the middle of the day and you'll be operating impulsively rather than from the sanctity of a heart seasoned by the sound of His reason.[1]

We all have a certain time of day when we function better, and it's important to have time with God when we are at our best. I happen to be a morning person, so mornings are the best for me. I get up early, when everything is still dark and before anything is stirring in the house, because that's the best time for me to meet God.

Martie and I laugh about the exaggerated fact that she wakes up in the morning one brain cell at a time—only if she has a mug of coffee in her hand! For her, meeting God in the middle of the morning, after I've gone to the office and her life is in order, works best. But maybe for others it's midday. For others, the best time to be with God might be eleven o'clock at night. Whenever it is, we need to give Him our best time. And we need to be careful not to make it a legalistic thing. If we miss having time with Him one day, we shouldn't feel guilty about it, because intimacy with God is more than a half-hour discipline. It's a daylong continual walk. But if we miss our time with God for three or four days, we may be in trouble.

Two psalms wonderfully illustrate the place that connecting to His Word and prayer play in our lives.

In Psalm 1 we read of the satisfying, sustaining, and securing work of God's Word in our lives. The psalmist tells us that when he has delighted in the law of the Lord instead of living in the counsel of the ungodly, his life has been like a tree planted by the rivers of water that bears fruit in season and whose leaves do not wither. Whatever he undertakes prospers. The contrast to the ungodly is clear. In their aloneness they are like the chaff—the worthless outer sheath of a kernel of wheat that is left to blow away in the wind.

The word for the condition of those who lose themselves in the Word of God is *blessed*. The psalmist begins the psalm by saying, "Blessed is the man." Blessed because he experiences the satisfaction that comes from a well-ordered life of a Word-led person. It is the blessing of lives that have meaning and purpose, that are clean and organized, that are driven by systems that ultimately satisfy. The choice in this psalm is clear. We find our lives being influenced either by the godless world in which we live or by the Word of God that enables us to live an abundant life.

Psalm 13 speaks to the stabilizing satisfaction that comes when we pray. At the beginning of this psalm, the psalmist is lost in despair. He complains that God has forgotten him and left him in a disastrous environment (vv. 1–4). But then the psalmist turns his heart toward God (v. 5). By the end of this brief psalm, God has not delivered him but instead has satisfied his soul in the midst of the distress (v. 6). The psalmist has experienced one of the most meaningful aspects of prayer: not the *answers* to prayer but the *way* in which prayer opens heaven for us to see God realistically and lose ourselves in a deep and unshaken confidence in the character of God. The psalmist closes this psalm, having transitioned from despair to delight, exclaiming,

> *I have trusted in Your lovingkindness;*
> *My heart shall rejoice in Your salvation.*
> *I will sing to the LORD,*
> *Because He has dealt bountifully with me (vv. 5–6).*

COMMUNICATING WITH GOD: PERSONAL TESTIMONIES

I have found several approaches to be helpful in connecting with God in my times of personal Bible study and prayer.

First, I must read the Word as a personal encounter with God. For me it cannot be just an exercise in reading through the Bible in a year or making sure I read a chapter a day or any other system I am trying to fulfill. Connecting with God in Scripture is just that—connecting personally with God. Each encounter must search for something from Him to me that is relevant to my life. I find that I need to read until He has spoken to me in a substantive way. If it comes quickly, I may not need to read further, though I may wish to read on. And if it takes more time than I had planned, I need to keep in the Word until there has been a ministry to my soul, heart, and mind.

Then I find that it is important to capture the ministry in a way that I can take with me through the day. Writing the concept down and putting it in my pocket, in my money clip, or in my briefcase so that I am confronted with it throughout the day is a big help in keeping the issue alive in my heart. Sometimes memorizing a key verse or making it a brief and memorable prayer that I can lift before Him throughout the day is a help as well.

Second, I find it helpful to read God's Word in terms of its intended purposes. This aligns me with what God wants to do in my life. He has told us that His word is a

- *Mirror:* Therefore I need to read to see myself as I really am in the light of what the text is saying.
- *Seed:* I permit the Word to be implanted deep in my heart and then envision what the fruit will be if I water and nurture it with care.
- *Sword:* The two-edged kind that pierces through all the externals and reveals the deepest secrets and motives. In this metaphor it is essential to let the Word cut where it will and to honestly admit and submit to its surgery.
- *Lamp:* It gives guidance and direction in the darkness of life.
- *Bread* for my soul: In this sense I need to let the Word of God nourish my soul through reading it to feed me, not just to inform me. When your soul is touched by a truth, encouragement, comfort, reproof, or insight from God's Word, it is a moment of feeding.

Third, I find it helpful to share with a trusted friend what God has given me from His Word for the day. This is especially productive if the friend is someone on the same spiritual wavelength as you. Sharing life-related insights can be a powerful tool in bonding not only with God but also with friends, your spouse, and your children.

Fourth, I often vary my approach to Scripture. For a season I may be reading two or three chapters a day in the Psalms and the proverb that goes with the day of the month. At other times a study of a theme (such as friends, money, love, repentance, forgiveness) using my concordance can be very enlightening, particularly if I am studying an area that I am struggling with in my own life. The biographies of Old Testament saints are full of stimulating food for connecting with God. Reading through a short New Testament book at one sitting may be helpful at another time in my pilgrimage. Whatever the approach, don't let yourself get bogged down in duty or artificial goals for your Bible study. Like any relationship, communication is most exhilarating when it doesn't keep talking about the same thing over and over. It's best when it centers on a point of need and interest.

Last, I must read the text submissively if I am to profit from its ability to connect me with the One who is speaking through it. Engaging the Word with less than an open, yielded spirit is a sure formula for an experience that will be distant and perfunctory. There is an old adage that appropriately says, "This book will keep you from sin or sin will keep you from this book!"

Prayer has a wonderful way of getting us to see all of life from God's point of view.

In regard to prayer, let me relate a couple of things that are helpful for me. Praying honestly is of utmost importance. The psalmist was never shy about getting in God's face about his life. This honesty opens our spirits up for Him to meet us with the resolution to our frustration. None of the psalms ever end with the psalmist still being ticked about life or God. Prayer has a wonderful way of getting us to see all of life from God's point of view.

Prayer must have elements of worship. This could be in the form of singing, gratitude, or communicating specific ways in which we express His worth in the coming day or situations. Needless to say, prayers of repentance and resolve are purifying and satisfying to our own souls and God.

I find that praying out loud helps me deal with a wandering mind. When my mind does wander, I often use it as an opportunity to pray for the situation or the person that my mind has drifted to—unless it's my golf game. That's hopeless.

Journaling prayers can also be a help to keep our hearts riveted.

Praying God's Word back to Him is a wonderful exercise in meaningful prayer. It not only helps us process His Word personally, but it lets God know that we have been paying attention and that we really do get it after all.

Most important, it is critical that we stay at it. There will be times when the exercise seems to be less exhilarating than you expect it to be. For a lot of reasons we don't always feel emotionally or spiritually sharp all the time. Don't abandon the process. Faithfulness is the key. Stay at it and your connectedness to God will deepen, and intimacy with Him will be your reward.

I realize that what works for me may not work for you. All of us have different ways of connecting with God in the Word and prayer. So I asked some of my friends whose spiritual lives I respect to share the ways they find to be effective in their progress toward intimacy with God. I asked them to respond briefly in three areas: (1) study of the Word of God, (2) prayer, and (3) other practices, such as meditation, memorization, journaling, or fasting. Below are their comments. (Some have been edited slightly.)

1. How and when do you study the Word of God?

Elizabeth Elliot Gren. I read the Bible nearly every day, usually early in the morning. I meditate on what I read, underline bits occasionally, and seek always to apply it in my daily life.

Bill Hybels. In the morning I read through books of the Bible in brief passages—reflect—apply them to my life. I do this through a journaling process, so that I write and record my thoughts, discoveries, and applications.

Joni Eareckson Tada. My personal study is always at home where it's quiet, unhurried, and where, when I ask the Spirit to guide me, I know there won't be interruptions of His still, small voice. For me, personal study involves this kind of reflection on His Word: I'll take each word of a verse and simply *think* through it.

The Lord is my Shepherd.

The *Lord* is my Shepherd.

The Lord *is* my Shepherd.

The Lord is *my* Shepherd.

The Lord is my *Shepherd.*

This kind of study requires no commentaries, no addendums, no cross-referencing, or the need of extra Bible helps. It is purely personal. The other kind of study I do—research on a topic—I will do at the office where I have an army of resources at my disposal. This kind of research/study is enormously beneficial to my "growing into the knowledge of the Lord," but it is not quite as intimate.

Kent Hughes. I often begin by refreshing myself as to the inspiration and authority of God's Holy Word by reciting 2 Timothy 3:16 and Jesus' words in Matthew 5:18 and Luke 4:4, combined with a reference to Deuteronomy 8:3: "But on every word that comes from the mouth of the Lord" (NIV). Next, I pray before I read the Word, asking for the ability to concentrate and listen to the Spirit. I then preview the section I am going to read. This is done by refreshing myself as to introductory matters—To whom was the book written? What is the purpose of the book?—and then I peruse the material before I read it. This method was inspired by Mortimer Adler's *How to Read a Book.*

For example, say I am going to read 1 Timothy. I note that it was written about AD 64 to encourage Timothy as he pastored a growing church in a confusingly decadent culture. I would also note that this was the eve of a Neroian persecution. But if I were reading 2 Timothy I would note that the persecution has begun. This accounts for the urgency and the strident material of some sections. This done, I would peruse the subject headings, getting a feel for where the book is going. Then I would read the book in one sitting. I normally put pencil marks in the margin by things I have noted, but I do not make annotations because I don't want to interrupt the flow of my reading. After reading the book, I go back and dwell on the places I have noted and then write notations, look up cross-references, and so on.

Crawford Loritts. As a rule, I read the Word first thing in the morning every day. I generally read sequentially through the Bible, from Genesis to Revelation, although not in a year's time. Occasionally I will look up a passage that relates to a particular burden I have that day. Also, I often read a proverb for that day or several psalms. Usually I do this within a twenty-minute time frame.

I make it a point to differentiate my personal reading of the Word from my study life. The time I spend preparing for specific sermons is a separate time.

Bill Bright.[2] As we have begun each day since we were married, Vonette and I get on our knees and acknowledge that Jesus Christ, who lives in our hearts, is the Lord of our lives and that He is the God-man, the One in whom dwells all the fullness of the godhead bodily, the One who is the visible expression of the invisible God, the One in whom we are complete.

After we have prayed together, I read the Word of God on my knees. That is my favorite position, because in so doing I am acknowledging my total dependence upon the Lord. I say something like: "Lord, please speak to me from Your holy, inspired, inerrant Word—Your divine truth. I know Your Holy Word is from Your own great loving heart. It is a love letter to me, and I want to understand what You have to say to me." I find this makes a vast difference than just sitting comfortably in a big, soft chair. I read the Bible in a spirit of reverence and worship and praise and thanksgiving. This daily spiritual practice is the most important discipline of the day.

It has been my practice for many years to read the Bible through the course of the year, by reading from the Old and New Testaments, the Psalms, and Proverbs each day.

Dr. Adrian Rogers. I study the Word of God by a simple reading and pondering of what I read. I almost always read with a pen in hand and try to analyze and outline what I read. When a particular truth comes out to me, I reflect on that truth and try to find amplification and application.

Jill Briscoe. I use Scripture Union notes for my personal devotions. (It's good not to be in the same area as teaching or writing.) I read and study every day "sometime." Seeing I am constantly on the run and on the road, I have no set time. I snatch the moment—an hour here and an hour there—so that I can "chew" on Scripture all day long.

2. How do you manage your prayer life? What works for you? What doesn't?

Elisabeth Elliot Gren. I begin with the ancient hymn (from about AD 300, I think), the *Te Deum*. Then I use the Lord's Prayer and other written prayers, including those contained in the great old hymns. Of course I have my own prayer lists: praise, thanksgiving, confession, intercession, etc.

Bill Hybels. I write out my prayers to God, longhand. It is the only way I can sustain focus and really organize my prayer in a balanced, meaningful way. Obviously, throughout my day, I just do "catch prayers."

Joni Eareckson Tada. My disability is my greatest asset in prayer because it forces me to bed early where, once I'm lying down, I have several hours to meditate, think, and reflect, sing hymns to the Lord, praise, intercede, offer thanksgiving and petition. It is the most wonderful "Mary" time for me, a "Martha." I don't know that if I were on my feet I'd have the discipline to carve out this amount of committed time in prayer—that is why I "boast in my affliction": it provides for me time which, otherwise, I might not devote to the Lord.

In my prayer time I use a lot of stanzas from favorite old hymns as fodder for faithful praying: "I Am His and He Is Mine," "May the Mind of Christ My Savior," "O Love That Will Not Let Me Go," and so many others. It's wonderful to sing to the Lord Jesus as though I were singing the song just for Him. It's the same feeling I had when, on my feet as a teenager, I used to play my piano in the living room and delight when Daddy would sneak in, find a comfortable chair, and just sit and listen to me. I was able to give a personal concert just for him.

Kent Hughes. Ephesians 6:18 gives the pattern I try to follow in my prayer life: "And pray in the Spirit on all occasions with all kinds of prayers and requests. With this in mind, be alert and always keep on praying for all the saints" (NIV). The believer whose prayer is *in-spirited* ("in the Spirit") has the indwelling Holy Spirit and the Word of God to guide him and to intercede for him. I try to keep in a *continual* attitude of prayer ("on all occasions") and to pray for the *varied* situations that come up throughout the day ("all kinds of prayers and requests").

Prayer needs to be *persistent* ("keep on praying"), and it should be *intercessory* ("for all the saints").

In my prayer notebook I include Scripture texts for *meditation, confession, submission,* and *adoration* (worship of God, celebration of His creatorship, the holiness of God, devotion to God, hymns of praise, and poetry of adoration). For *petitionary* or *intercessory* prayer, I've found it helpful to keep a prayer list with different pages for a variety of concerns. The list is divided into daily and weekly petitions. Barbara and I pray for family members, those who are ill, personal requests, personal life, evangelism, ministry colleagues, work, the world, Christian leaders, and government leaders, to name a few. We pray together daily—and have a more lengthy time of prayer on my day off. We especially pray for our children and our concerns for them. Prayer needs to take place where you can be undisturbed and when you are at your best. Prayer is work—if you wait until you "feel" like praying, you will never really keep at it.

Crawford Loritts. I have developed the habit of writing prayer letters to the Lord every day. (My wife says this has become a fire hazard due to the stacks of paper in the closet!) I have a prayer list I don't get through every day, but I usually go through the whole list three times a week.

Within the last nine months, I made a commitment to God that I would talk to Him each day before talking to anyone else, including my wife. I pray in four main areas: (1) for cleansing and purity in God's presence; (2) that my family will experience God's power and touch; (3) that I will have wisdom and direction in whatever major assignment is facing me that day; (4) and general worship, thanksgiving, and praise.

Each day after dropping my kids off at school, I go to the same restaurant where I read the Word, write my prayer letter, and pray through my prayer list. Four times a week I take a thirty-minute walk and use the time to pray for future generations—my children, grandchildren, etc.

Once a month I go away to a special place to spend time with the Lord. I get away from phones and faxes, listening to God and the impressions He gives through His Word and the Holy Spirit. I seek God's priorities and seek to make adjustments in my life.

Through the course of each day I am conscious that my whole life is an issue of prayer. I try not to go through any meeting or appointment without prayer. It's an ongoing process in my life.

Bill Bright. For many years my prayer life has been a discipline of practicing the presence of God. I try to remain in a spirit of prayer "without ceasing" throughout the day, whether I am speaking, in a meeting, or whatever I may be doing. I have found that I can maintain a divine communication with the Lord Himself throughout the day. I don't mean to say that there is a perfect "connection" every minute, twenty-four hours a day, but that is my desire. It is a beautiful and intimate kind of relationship.

I do not think of prayer as a legalistic discipline—that I must spend a prescribed number of minutes or hours each day on my knees in prayer. But as I begin my day, my first conscious thoughts are of Him, and all day long, until I lose consciousness at night, my thoughts are on Him. At bedtime, Vonette and I are again on our knees together to praise Him, to worship Him, and to thank Him for guiding our steps during the day.

Dr. Adrian Rogers. My prayer life is something I have never been satisfied with but will forever be grateful for. God is real to me, and I have no difficulty talking to Him in the closet or as I go. I try to greet the Lord every morning with praise, receptivity, and surrender before I get into anything else. This is a practice even before I get to any devotional time.

After a bath and breakfast, Joy and I have a time together where we generally read from Oswald Chambers, pray for our children and grandchildren by name, pray for one another, pray for friends and family who have needs, and then pray for a particular section of the world. On Mondays we pray for Mexico and the Caribbean; on Tuesdays we pray for South America; on Wednesdays we pray for Africa; on Thursdays we pray for Europe; on Fridays we pray for the Middle East; and on Saturdays we pray for the Far East. Then comes Sunday, when we pray for America, for political leaders, and for national spiritual leaders.

Somewhere I read about Dwight L. Moody, where it was said that he never made long prayers and he was never long without prayer. When I read that, I thought that sounds so much like what I practice. I try to pray for things as they come up, for people before I meet them and after I meet them, for people to whom I am writing, and even for pastors when I read their church bulletins.

Jill Briscoe. I try to pray "all the time" (without ceasing). I try to practice praying for people as I meet them face to face throughout the day—even while talking to them. I plan to get up really early for seasons of prayer.

3. Do you follow any additional practices, such as meditation, memorization, journaling, or fasting?

Elisabeth Elliot Gren. I have kept journals for fifty-three years. My husband and I usually fast each week.

Bill Hybels. Solitude is a regular practice at least one hour per day—often more. Journaling almost every day. Fasting only occasionally. Celebration—often. Deep fellowship and sharing—often. Secret acts of service—regularly.

Bill Bright. As I dictate this, Vonette and I together are in the thirty-eighth day of our most recent forty-day fast. I assure you that my prayer life is incredibly enhanced by fasting. The Lord has led me through four forty-day fasts.

Fasting with prayer is truly a spiritual atomic bomb in its potential. No other Christian discipline meets the conditions of 2 Chronicles 7:14 as does fasting. There is something about God's Holy Spirit wooing us and blessing us into that great heart of God Himself as we seek His face with broken and contrite spirits.

I also place a strong emphasis on memorization. Memorizing Scripture is one of the most important things one can do, and I strongly encourage it. Keeping a journal is also a wonderful way to record thoughts, ideas, or strategies that come to us as we pray and meditate on the Lord, and which may be from the Holy Spirit.

Crawford Loritts. Sometimes I fast when I feel led of the Lord to do so, usually relating to a particular burden. Sometimes the fasts involve going without things other than food, such as not watching a game or doing something else I would like to do.

I do Bible memory with my kids. I lead them in a Bible study each week that involves memory verses.

Dr. Adrian Rogers. I meditate much on Scripture. I try to take a verse of Scripture to bed with me each night and think it out as I go to sleep. I have memorized quite a bit of Scripture but not by trying—only by use. I do very little journaling, and fast from time to time. I intend to fast more.

Jill Briscoe. My journaling turns into books! I fast regularly—whenever family gatherings are happening and in times of crisis. I fast for our children more than anyone else. Fasting keeps my prayers focused on what God wants me to pray about.

MAX LUCADO ON BIBLE STUDY

Max Lucado's response took the form of a short lesson on Bible study.

A friend of mine married an opera soprano. She loves concerts. Her college years were spent in the music department, and her earliest memories are of keyboards and choir risers. He, on the other hand, leans more toward Monday Night Football and country music. He also loves his wife, so, on occasion, he attends an opera. The two sit side by side in the same auditorium, listening to the same music with two completely different responses. He sleeps and she weeps.

I believe the difference is more than taste. It is training. She has spent hours learning to appreciate the art of music. He has spent none. Her ears are Geiger-counter sensitive. He can't differentiate between staccato and fortissimo. But he is trying. Last time we talked about the concerts, he was managing to stay awake. He might never have the same ear as his wife, but he can learn.

I believe we can, too. Equipped with the right tools, we can learn to have a fruitful daily appointment with God. What are those tools? Here are the ones I have found helpful.

1. *Have a regular time and place.* Select a slot on your schedule and corner of your world and claim it for God. For some of you, it may be best to do this in the morning. "In the morning my prayer comes before

You" (Psalm 88:13). Others prefer the evening and agree with David's prayer: "May my prayer be set before you like incense; may the lifting up of my hands be like the evening sacrifice" (Psalm 141:2 NIV). Others prefer many encounters during the day. Apparently the author of Psalm 55 did. He wrote, "Evening, morning and noon I cry out" (v. 17 NIV).

Some sit under a tree, others in the kitchen. Maybe your commute to work or your lunch break would be appropriate. Find a time and place that seems right for you.

How much time should you take? My advice would be to value the quality of the encounter over the length of the encounter. At the risk of oversimplifying the matter, I suggest that your quiet time last long enough for you to say what you want and God to say what He wants.

2. *Bring an open Bible.* God speaks to you through His Word. The first step in reading the Bible is to ask God to help you understand it. "But the Helper, the Holy Spirit, whom the Father will send in My name, He will teach you all things, and bring to your remembrance all that I said to you" (John 14:26). Before reading the Bible, pray. Don't go to Scripture looking for *your* idea; go searching for *His*. Read the Bible prayerfully.

Read the Bible carefully. Jesus told us: "Seek, and you will find" (Matthew 7:7). God commends those who "chew on Scripture day and night" (Psalm 1:2 THE MESSAGE). The Bible is not a newspaper to be skimmed but rather a mine to be quarried. If you look in the Bible for wisdom the way you would search a mine for silver, and if you would read the Bible for understanding the way you would hunt for hidden treasure, you will understand respect for the Lord and will find that you know God (see Proverbs 2:4–5 NIV).

Study the Bible a little at a time. Choose depth over amount. Read until a verse "hits" you, then stop and meditate. Copy the verse onto a sheet of paper or write it into your journal and reflect back on it several times.

On a recent morning my quiet time found me in Matthew 18. I was only four verses into the chapter when I read, "The greatest [person] in the kingdom of heaven" is the one who "humbles himself [like] this little child" (NKJV). I needed go no further. I copied the words in my journal and pondered them on and off during the day. I asked myself, *How can I be more childlike?* I asked God, *Make me kinder today, gentler today.*

Will I learn what God intends? If I listen, I will. God seems to send messages like He did His manna, one day's portion at a time. He provides "a command here, a command there. A rule here, a rule there. A little lesson here, a little lesson there" (Isaiah 28:10, author's paraphrase).

Don't be discouraged if your reading reaps a small harvest. Some days a lesser portion is all we need. A little girl returned from her first day at school. Her mom asked, "Did you learn anything?" "Apparently not enough," the girl responded. "I have to go back tomorrow and the next day and the next day . . ."

Such is the case with learning. And such is the case with Bible study. Understanding comes a little at a time over a lifetime.

3. *Have an open heart.* Don't forget the admonition from James: "The one who looks steadily at God's perfect law and makes that his habit— not listening and then forgetting, but actively putting it into practice— will be happy in all that he does" (James 1:25, author's paraphrase).

You know you are connecting when what you read in the Bible is what others see in your life. Perhaps you've heard the story of the not-so-bright fellow who saw the advertisement for a cruise. The sign in the travel agency window read "Cruise—$100 cash."

I've got a hundred dollars, he thought. *And I'd like to go on a cruise.* So he entered the door and announced his desires. The fellow at the desk asked for the money and the not-too-bright guy started counting it out. When he got to one hundred he was whacked over the head and knocked out. He woke up in a barrel floating down a river. Another guy in another barrel floated past and asked him, "Say, do they serve lunch on this cruise?"

"They didn't last year."

It's one thing not to know. It's another to know and not learn. Paul urged his readers to put into practice what they had learned from him. "What you have learned and received and heard and seen in me, do" (Philippians 4:9 RSV).

Communicating with God in these kinds of ways is foundational to intimacy. It's the prerequisite. As we stay in this kind of fellowship, then all other points at which we connect will be strengthened as well.

CONNECTING WITH GOD'S CHARACTER AND CONDUCT

When we spend time with God in prayer and in His Word, we connect to God's character and conduct. God's Word details what He is really like and how He actually operates. Prayer enables us to see Him clearly and be reminded of His character and ways. By faith we hold onto the reality of His unchanging personality. We can hang on by faith to the fact that when our whole world is rejecting us and we feel marginalized and lonely, He cares for us because He is a loving God. It's not because of us, thankfully, but because it's intrinsic to His character. He can't help but love and care for us because He cannot deny Himself.

> *When we spend time with God in prayer and in His Word, we connect to God's character and conduct.*

In times of chaos we know we can connect with His sovereignty because we know that He works under the surface of chaos and manages it to be all that is good and gain.

Martie and I had the privilege of taking a trip that included a visit to Hong Kong. It was my pleasure to spend a couple of hours one morning with a young man who had just escaped from communist China. He had been jailed there for his faith. His story resonated with the fact that when we connect to God by faith and endure in times of difficulty, His sovereign ability to overrule the systems that control and surround our lives to bring them to His gain and glory is compellingly real.

This young man was a student at one of the universities in China and had bought into the student revolt that ultimately led to the June 1989 bloody massacre in Tiananmen Square. He told me that that student uprising had captured the hearts of students in China. It was the singular focus of their lives, the only meaning and purpose for their existence. Their dream was to bring about change in the Chinese culture.

I'll never forget reading about the student revolt from afar. In my mind, I knew that if they were successful, there was a good chance that China would open to the gospel. What a thrilling prospect! But I still recall that when I saw the tanks roll into Tiananmen Square and crush rebellion, they crushed the hope of my own heart that the gospel could be free in China.

I was wrong.

This young man related to me that after Tiananmen Square many of his friends committed suicide. They were stripped of hope and had nothing to live for. It was that way all across China on every university campus, he said. He himself felt the depth of despair and emptiness that the loss of meaning and purpose had brought. One of the English teachers he had before Tiananmen Square was a Christian. The students mocked this teacher and told him he was a fool to believe that there was a God. But now, in the emptiness of his heart, this Chinese student went back to that teacher and asked him about the God he so clearly embraced. This young man then accepted Christ as his personal Savior, as did his girlfriend, who was soon to become his wife. He went on and finished at the university and found himself in a fellowship group of other Christian students.

He was assigned to teach at one of the leading universities where government officials were trained. As he taught there, he took the opportunity to share his faith with others and soon had a growing and dynamic fellowship of believers around him. He told me that they used to have parties at nearby hotels, and all the Christians would invite their friends. During the party Christians would spontaneously get up and tell how Christ had changed their lives. When others would accept Christ they would lock the doors and take them into the shower and baptize them on the spot. Soon the government officials found out and threw this young professor into prison.

As he unfolded the story of his life and how he came to Christ, he related to me that there is not a university in China that doesn't have a thriving group of Christian students. Bewildered, I asked him how that came to be. He told me that as it was in his life, so it was with hundreds and now thousands of other students, who, having lost all hope at Tiananmen Square, turned their hope to Jesus Christ.

What a dramatic move by God.

As I listened, I was struck afresh with what a marvelous God we have and how that, even in the midst of what seems like the worst to us, we can experience in our hearts the reality of a God who works all things together for good. This experience, even though it didn't happen to me, filled my heart with satisfaction and renewed in me the sense of being sustained and secured in any circumstance in life.

Intimacy is deepened when we experience the reality of who He is and how He conducts His divine affairs in and around our lives. But that requires that we intentionally by faith live in the reality of all that He is and does. Intimacy develops when we connect with His unfailing righteousness, mercy, grace, justice, all-surpassing wisdom, power, and protection. It is about trusting that His ways are best and waiting with hearts that anticipate how He will reveal His marvelously consistent character and conduct in and around our lives.

CONNECTING WITH GOD IN CREATION

Psalm 19:1 says, "The heavens are telling of the glory of God." We need "to stop and smell the roses," as the saying goes. But we can't just love the roses and what they mean to us when we get a dozen in the mail. We need to stop living on the secondary level, the creation, and move to the loftier one as we are struck with the wonder of the Almighty God who could craft and design something so intricate and beautiful.

Look at the sky filled with stars and think of Christ the Creator. Bask in the reality that the One who formed all of this vast expanse that is known as the universe by the Word of His mouth is your creator and friend. Contemplate the sun rising in the morning, which gives us just enough heat to sustain us—not so much that it burns us and not so little that we freeze to death. As we see Christ as the source, we get in touch with Him and appreciate afresh His power and wisdom.

Colonel Guy Gardner, an astronaut, tells of his experiences in the Moody Video production *Planet Earth*. Speaking of the marvels of creation he saw in space, he paused and, with tears welling in his eyes, said, "It's very hard to think this must have happened by chance . . . You realize at the same time that there had to be a Master Designer, a Creator, of this planet. And to me that makes life all the more special. Because that tells me that instead of me being something that just came along in the course of time to live and die, that instead of a meaningless existence, I have Someone—who cares for me—who has made me—and cares about me. Someone I can go to with my troubles, and my cares, and my joys."

> *It's hard to feel far from God when we see Him in all that is around us.*

It's hard to feel far from God when we see Him in all that is around us.

CONNECTING WITH GOD IN WORSHIP AND PRAISE

Psalm 22:3 says that the Lord inhabits the praises of His people. That's a good thing for us to know. Too often the church is simply a community of grumpy old murmuring and complaining saints. Is it any wonder that God seems far away?

When we praise Him, however, with grateful, humble, adoring hearts, we connect. In fact, worship is more than singing—it is serving in ways that express His worth to us. The writer of the book of Hebrews exhorts us, "Through Him then, let us continually offer up a sacrifice of praise to God, that is, the fruit of lips that give thanks to His name. And do not neglect doing good and sharing, for with such sacrifices God is pleased" (13:15–16). Lives that worship like this are lives that position themselves to be in touch with God.

CONNECTING WITH GOD IN CRISIS

James 1 says that when trouble comes we should count it all joy, because God will meet us there. He will use that problem to shape, mold, and frame us and to knock off the rough edges of our lives. The text tells us we need to lie still while God, who is the Divine Surgeon, works in our lives. We need to be steadfast in times of crisis and by faith connect with His grace and feel His sustaining power. It's during these times that we experience the fullness of His grace. Throughout my years as a pastor, I have had people tell me time and again, "I can't believe how buoyed I feel by God. Without Him I wouldn't make it through this time in my life." That's a brush with intimacy that we rarely feel on Easy Street.

Do you think that Shadrach, Meshach, and Abednego were more intimately connected with God before or after their furnace experience? When they went through the crisis of the furnace, God met them there. They became intimately connected to Him in the midst of the fire, and they never forgot it. That is why James says that when troubles come we shouldn't resist them as enemies but instead welcome them as friends. We meet God in unusual and powerful ways in the midst of crisis. In fact, one of the reasons He permits trouble in our lives is to give us an opportunity to go more deeply with Him and to experience Him more fully. If you want to know God more intimately, look for Him in the furnace of your life.

CONNECTING WITH GOD IN OBEDIENCE

The striking metaphor in the text on the vine and the branches in John 15 tells us that we have the privilege of becoming intimately entwined with Him. The branches are not just stuck on the vine; they are intimately infused into it. The concept of abiding involves my finally, fully, yielding myself to Him as my source. He will sustain, satisfy, and secure my life as an extension of His life, which is the vine. Every time we obey, we put ourselves on a track where God will meet us, commune with us, and manage the environment around us to reveal Himself and His ways. When we obey without condition or qualification, we position ourselves to experience Him and His ways. In giving, we experience His provision. In righteous living, we experience His peace and presence. In sacrifice and suffering, we experience His grace and enablement. As we obey, He satisfies, secures, and sustains.

Many of us struggle with bitterness and then wonder why God is not close. God walks paths of forgiveness. He is never seen on paths of revenge and hate. If we are greedy instead of generous, angry instead of patient, complacent instead of compassionate, self-centered instead of serving, we will not know the joy of nearness to Him. He walks in unusual places, and intimacy is about being obediently found in the way with Him.

A PRODIGAL'S PROGRESS

When the Prodigal realized how bad things were for him in the far country, he took the one obvious and essential step: He returned to his father. He did what it took to be restored to face-to-face contact with him.

We cannot see God during our sojourn on this earth, but we *can* place ourselves in proximity to Him. So, as we have noted, we can do this through prayer, the study of His Word, worship, praise, obedience, purity in our conduct and speech, and acknowledging His creative power and holy character. Intimacy involves knowing who we are and how much we need God; it involves desiring to connect with Him simply to please Him, and then, by faith, plugging in.

There isn't one of us who needs to remain connectedly challenged. Is anyone tired of life without God? Is anyone tired of the satisfaction of sin for a season, only to feel its hollowness and guilt? Is there anyone who would rather have a Savior than the sin? Is there anyone who is tired of the aloneness in his or her soul, who would like to lean toward intimacy and begin to connect to the only One who satisfies and sustains and secures?

Then get in touch.

Don't let go.

Regardless of what happens.

nine

INTIMACY IN THE TRENCHES

Finding Rest in a Day of Crisis

I KNOW THAT YOU CAN DO ALL THINGS,
AND THAT NO PURPOSE OF YOURS CAN BE THWARTED.
JOB 42:2

Connecting to God as an everyday matter of routine faithfulness prepares us for being connected to Him in times of crisis. When life takes us to the ragged edge of reality, the intimacy we have developed with God will take us through with hands held high in victory.

One Sunday after I preached at a morning church service in Dallas, a nice-looking man and his family came up to me afterward and told me how the last three years had brought tremendous trauma into their lives. He had been very successful at business, but suddenly it all collapsed and he lost nearly everything. Some of his competitors had filed unfair litigation against him, which had been in process for almost three years and was still unresolved.

In the midst of this, a friend of his from Phoenix called him by phone and said, "Bob, remember 46:10." "What do you mean?" Bob asked. His friend simply replied, "I'm going to send you something in the mail, but until you get it, just remember 46:10." Bob wondered if maybe that would be the year all of his problems would be solved! Or, being from Dallas, he wondered if it was an audible called at the line by the quarterback of the Dallas Cowboys.

Two days later he received a UPS package. In it was a big wooden plaque with an inscription on a brass plate: "46:10."

As he turned the plaque over, Bob saw that on the back was written the verse: "Be still, and know that I am God . . . Psalm 46:10" (KJV).

LIVING OUT PSALM 46:10

What do you do when God takes you all the way out to the ragged edge of reality? Life has a way of doing that, and none of us is exempt. The issue here is not the ordinary problems in our lives we can control and fix. It's those times in our lives when we no longer have the resources to do anything about what we face. We can only stand back and watch.

If you asked me what to do in these times of crisis, I would say *relax!* Just relax! And you would say, "Stowell, you've never been to the ragged edge of reality, because if you'd ever been out there, you would know that you don't just relax."

But Psalm 46 says just that. If you asked God what to do when you're at the ragged edge of reality, He would say "Relax!" Psalm 46 wraps itself around one central statement in verse 10: "Cease striving and know that I am God."

> God says that when we get out to the ragged edge, we have to let go.

I grew up hearing the King James Version of the verse, "Be still, and know that I am God." But I always thought that meant just to "be still," like my mother always used to say to me in church (I still have the imprints on my knees from her hands where she squeezed them as she firmly said, "Joe, would you please *be still?*") So I grew up thinking that the verse meant basically to stop wiggling and listen to God—until I began to study the text and discovered that the Hebrew word used for "be still" has nothing to do with rapt attention to God. Rather, it has everything to do with relaxing. In fact, the verse could be translated literally as "Relax, and know that I am God."

The Hebrew word paints a vivid picture. It means to *let go.* When life takes us to the ragged edge, we always want to keep our hands on the problem and manipulate it and seek to control it and force it to the outcome we want. We are like little children who always want to get involved in projects with their parent. (I don't know why it is that when kids are too young to help they *want* to help, but when they're older and more capable, they are no longer interested!)

God says that when we get out to the ragged edge, we have to let go. We need to give up controlling, manipulating, and striving to somehow make it work. If we don't, we'll usually just make things worse.

The Hebrew word also means to let go, to put our hands down at our sides. In times of struggle we usually want to defend or protect ourselves. Putting our hands down at our sides makes us feel vulnerable. But that's what God is saying here. He's saying that we need to stop striving, let go, put our hands down, take a deep breath, and relax.

If that's all God told us to do, it would probably be impossible. But thankfully, the psalm goes on to give us the process for doing this. The only way we can relax is to know something about God. As the verse says, "Cease striving and *know* . . ." Normally we don't connect our responses to knowing but rather to feeling. We are most often motivated in a crisis by our emotions—that wave of anxiety or surge of self-pity. Our emotions often form and drive our response. But notice that God says the only way we are going to be able to relax is to start with something we know, to start with a cognitive reality that is steady and stable.

I think my all-time favorite sporting event was back in 1980 when the Winter Olympics were held at Lake Placid, New York. The Olympics were held during a time when America was in malaise, as former President Jimmy Carter put it. Those were bad days for the country. The Cold War was at its height, and Russia seemed so powerful and the United States so weak. Americans were being held hostage in Iran, and when we sent troops to rescue them, the planes ended up crashing in the desert in a sandstorm. In the midst of all of this, we had to host the Winter Olympics, when all those Europeans who lived in ice and snow were going to come and shame us again—especially when it came to playing hockey. (This was back in the days when professional athletes could not play in the Olympics, so the United States had to find its best college players and field them against those genetically engineered Russians!)

I remember the Sunday we played hockey against the Russians. After church, Martie and I came home with the kids, and Martie went into the kitchen to fix dinner while I, like every good husband, stayed out of the kitchen, grabbed a remote, and sprawled out on the couch.

(That was before Promise Keepers, so don't hold it against me!) I turned on the TV to see how the game was progressing, and I couldn't believe it—the U.S. team was ahead. As I watched the players skating, I wondered if it was really possible that we had a chance to beat the Russians. My stomach was in a knot. I had paid for the whole couch, but that afternoon I used only the front edge! In the third period the U.S. was still ahead. I knew the Russians would score five goals in the last five minutes and wreck everything. I was wrong. When the buzzer sounded, we had beaten the Russians!

It was such a big deal that the game was replayed on national television that evening. So Martie and I popped some popcorn and turned on the game to watch it. This time the experience was totally different. We sat back and used the whole couch and enjoyed our popcorn and Pepsi. I put my feet up and never felt a twinge of anxiety. It was the same game, same sequence, same players, same ice, same everything. What made the difference? The difference lay in what I knew.

While Psalm 46 doesn't say we can relax because we know the outcomes, it does say that relaxing comes from knowing the One who *manages* the outcomes. And actually it's better to know and trust the God of the outcomes than to know the outcomes themselves. If we knew the outcome, we might forget the God who manages them and disagree with Him on the implementation. When we know God for all that He is and is able to do, we will have the capacity to turn it over to Him and let go, put our hands down, take a deep breath, and relax.

For me, the ragged edge of reality is shopping for cards. As I was looking for an anniversary card for Martie, I noticed on another shelf a box with a tantalizing picture of a mound of Oreo cookies surrounding a big glass of milk, with sweat running down the glass. I was galvanized toward the picture and wondered what was in the box. I went over and grabbed it off the shelf. It was a five-hundred-piece jigsaw puzzle.

I've already admitted that I'm really not into jigsaw puzzles. They remind me of nursing homes where half-done jigsaw puzzles sit on tables so people on their way to dinner can stop by and put in a couple more pieces, like a community project. But at this particular moment, the marketplace seduced me. I had to buy the puzzle because the picture was so compelling. I even thought that it might pass for a great anniversary gift, since Martie is addicted to things like Oreo cookies and chocolate! When I got home we opened the box and threw the pieces out on a table. What had been such a beautiful picture on the box was now only a bunch of disconnected, upside-down pieces.

Sometimes life feels like that. And if all we have are the pieces on the tabletop, we have no hope. But then we remember the box top. It and it alone makes sense of the mess. Psalm 46 tells us that God is in a sense the "box top" of our lives. When we know Him we have the assurance that there is order and meaning under the chaos and that all things will work out for His glory and our good in the end.

This concept of "knowing God" needs some definition. If we aren't careful, we may think of Him as an ethereal cloud of divine dust particles wafting through the universe, and we pray that someday He'll pass by close enough for us to see and feel Him. But the wonderful thing about God is that He is "solid." In a sense, He has "handles" on Him. We can "get our hands" on God. We can grab onto specific realities about Him and then hang onto those realities throughout our lives. There are some things that are absolutely, fully, finally true about God, and when we know and cling to what is true about God, we can relax and let Him do the work.

Before we examine those realities, it's useful to remember that Psalm 46 came out of a particular historical moment in the life of the nation of Israel. Second Chronicles 20:1 explains the situation. "Now it came about . . . that the sons of Moab and the sons of Ammon, together with some of the Meunites, came to make war against Jehoshaphat." This is a very interesting cluster of names. They identify the three most powerful military nations at the time—and those nations were linked by treaty against Jehoshaphat. For him this truly was the ragged edge of reality.

It's also interesting to note that Jehoshaphat was one of Judah's righteous kings. In all of his years, we are told, he walked in the ways of the Lord, as did his father, Asa (v. 32). That's important, because some of us think that the only people who get thrown out to the ragged edge are those who deserve it, people who have done terrible things, and that God is going to straighten them out by putting them out on the edge. I'm not saying that God doesn't do that sometimes, but it's not always the case. In fact, I think it's more often the case that godly, righteous people end up on the ragged edge. Jehoshaphat was a righteous man up against a situation over which he had no control. He did not have the military might to even dream of surviving. If he went to battle against them, in human terms, he'd be finished.

I love the honesty of verse 3, which says that Jehoshaphat "was afraid." It doesn't say that since he was a man of God he stood up and felt really strong in his situation. No, he felt the same kind of fear we do when we find ourselves out on the ragged edge—anxiety and fear and living twenty-four hours a day with a knot in the stomach.

But notice what verse 3 says next about Jehoshaphat: He "turned his attention to seek the LORD."

This is instructive. When we are on the ragged edge of reality, how should we respond? When Jehoshaphat was afraid, he knew exactly what to do. He turned his attention toward God. For some of us, God is the last place we go. It's easier to blame Him than to trust Him when life goes bad.

Now let's go back to Psalm 46 and put some "handles" on God to which we can cling when life is beyond our control. In verse 1 we see three categories about the reality of God in the midst of trouble, and a fourth is in verse 10. Number one is that we *know* that *God is willing to spend His power on us.* "God is our refuge and strength." Notice the personal pronoun. It doesn't just say that God is a refuge but that He is *our* refuge. We *know* that God is willing to *protect* us when we're out on the ragged edge. He builds fences and hedges around us.

Not only does he spend His power and protection on us but also we *know* that He is present with us. As Psalm 46:1 puts it, He is a "very present help in trouble." In verses 7 and 11 we are told that "the LORD of hosts is with us; [He] is our stronghold." He is present with us and helps us by supplying His grace, as He did for Paul when he had a thorn in the flesh. This thorn was something Paul could not conquer; it was beyond him and troubled him all the time. Paul said that during that time he found that God's grace was sufficient (2 Corinthians 12:9). God helps us and gives us the strength to get through.

Think about the life of Joseph. Time and again he found himself at the ragged edge. Although he was a good, righteous young man, he was thrown into a pit by his brothers and then sold into slavery in Egypt. There his master's wife tried daily to seduce him. When he refused her, she falsely accused him, and he was thrown into prison. Joseph's problems didn't end there, but throughout all his ragged-edge experiences, God was with him. The account in Genesis of Joseph's life is punctuated with the phrase, "The LORD was with him" (Genesis 39:3, 23; cf. Acts 7:9).

We can also *know* that *God will be exalted in our dilemma*, as the psalmist declares at the end of verse 10: "[God] will be exalted among the nations." God's reputation rides on the ragged-edge realities of life. In a world full of people who aren't His, we stick out like sore thumbs. If we've been honest about our faith, most people know that we belong to God, and they are watching whenever we move out to the ragged edge of reality to see how we respond and what God will do with us there.

What does God do for us in these times? We have to remember that He said that He will be exalted, that He will not waste our sorrow, that He will not let us just shrivel and die out there. He will be exalted in our lives. That may not come today; it may not even come next year; and it may not come until the other side, when we get home. But God will prove the point, and He will be exalted in our difficulties. He will never allow something into our lives He cannot transition to glory, the gain of His kingdom, and our ultimate good. Throughout Scripture, God not only claims this truth but also proves it. We can relax and know God, put our arms down, and take a deep breath.

I think it's interesting to see how God resolved Jehoshaphat's problem. Jehoshaphat called together the whole assembly of Judah.

> *Then in the midst of the assembly the Spirit of the LORD came upon Jahaziel the son of Zechariah, the son of Benaiah, the son of Jeiel, the son of Mattaniah, the Levite of the sons of Asaph; and he said, "Listen, all Judah and the inhabitants of Jerusalem and King Jehoshaphat: thus says the LORD to you, 'Do not fear or be dismayed because of this great multitude, for the battle is not yours but God's'"* (2 Chronicles 20:14–15).

The three armies were still out there threatening the Israelites, and the Israelites knew they had to arm themselves for battle against them the next day. But I find it interesting that they didn't start chewing their nails and sharpening their swords. Instead, Jahaziel the prophet encouraged the people by reminding them that the battle was the Lord's and the outcome was in His control. They called in the singers and had a worship service!

Think how unique this is. One would think that a worship service would take place after God had resolved the problem. When was the last time you and I, in the midst of a ragged-edge experience, lifted our voices in praise to God for what He would do? But that's the Psalm 46:10 principle. The people focused on what they knew to be true about God, and their knowledge resulted in hearts full of praise. They praised Him before the resolution ever came.

> *When God finally takes care of our problems, we can be assured that it will be done the best way.*

The next morning they got up and obeyed God. They gathered their army and went out to face their enemies. I have to say, however, that the military strategy Jehoshaphat followed that morning as he arranged his forces seems somewhat naïve to me. If I were going out against those armies, I would have put my crack troops at the front to try to do as much damage as soon as possible. But Jehoshaphat put the singers at the front. As his troops marched to the precipice where they were to meet the opposing armies, the musicians marched before them, singing praises to God.

Don't you love the refreshing difference about the way they handled life at the ragged edge? A worship service followed by obedience. Then take a look at the outcome. During the preceding night, God sent marauding groups of mercenaries to ambush the three armies who had come together against them. The armies woke up to face these bandits, and in the darkness they ended up destroying each other. When Jehoshaphat's troops got to the edge of the precipice and looked down into the valley, they saw the three mighty armies all dead. Not one of them had escaped.

When God finally takes care of our problems, we can be assured that it will be done the best way. Nor will anything be undone. The battle is not ours. It is the Lord's.

For Jehoshaphat and Judah, trusting, worshiping, and obeying put them in a place where God could reveal Himself in intimate and dramatic ways.

MEASURING OUR SPIRITUAL BLOOD PRESSURE

How can we take a spiritual blood pressure test in the midst of anxiety? How do we know if we are spiritually relaxed? Psalm 46 and its historical background give us at least four measurements we use to track how well we're doing.

Number one is the Jehoshaphat response: *turn our face to the Lord.* We can either turn our faces to the Lord and put our arms down and acknowledge that He is in control, or we can turn our backs to Him and lean on our own capacities—and finally give ourselves ulcers and high blood pressure and anxiety and despair and hopelessness. When we turn our faces to the Lord, it's sign number one that we are beginning the process of relaxing. The longer we look at His face and His grand powers, the smaller our problems look. There isn't a problem in life that is bigger than God.

The second measure is that when we look to Him *we must believe.* Why would Jehoshaphat command the singers to have a worship service before they ever went to battle? Because he believed what he knew to be true about God. The prophet had said, "The battle is not yours but God's." Jehoshaphat believed that the outcome was safe in God's hands.

The third measure is that *we must praise God in the midst of our difficulties.* That doesn't mean that tears aren't running down our cheeks or our hearts aren't broken or we're not feeling the pressures of our problems. God doesn't promise to release us from the symptoms of our problems. He promises to be there with us and to see us all the way through. With quivering lips in the midst of the pain we praise Him. We say that

He is good, that we are trusting Him, and that He will see us through. It's a worship service regardless, for we have turned our faces toward Him in belief.

Fourth, *we will be faithful.* Faithful even in the tough assignments God gives to us. God told Jehoshaphat to advance toward the enemy at daybreak. Jehoshaphat and his men faithfully obeyed even though it might have meant annihilation.

It's easy for us to be unfaithful in the time of trouble. If some enemy or other person has caused trouble in our lives, it's easy to respond with vengeance, hatred, and bitterness toward them. Faithfulness calls us to the tough task of forgiveness. When life takes us to the ragged edge, it is easy to be unfaithful to God and lose trust in His character. It's easy to doubt that He is good anymore. It's easy to believe He doesn't care. It's easy to feel abandoned by Him. Yet staying connected means that we never stop clinging to Him regardless of our instincts to the contrary. Faithfulness means we are willing to suffer for God's sake if necessary in the midst of trouble.

Being faithful means staying connected to God, clinging to Him in such a way that disloyalty never actualizes itself in our choices.

Turning to God . . . believing in Him . . . praising Him . . . being faithful to Him. This is how we can know if we have learned to be still and know that He is God. This is what intimacy in the trenches is all about.

I have to add a word of caution here. We need to remember that we're trusting God to manage the outcomes, and that means that He manages the *timing.* We may think that if we keep in line with the four measurements and learn to relax and stay connected, that by Monday all our troubles will be resolved. It was nice for Jehoshaphat that his season of stress was short. Second Chronicles 20 is a short-stress, happily-ever-after story. Sometimes it works like that. But sometimes it doesn't.

I'm convinced that Job never fully understood why he had to experience so much trouble for such a long period of time. He suffered for no earthly good but rather suffered for God's reputation in the universe. Satan slandered God by saying that He wasn't worthy of a man's praise unless He had "bought" him by blessing his life. He challenged God to take away all the things He had done for Job and see if Job would be faithful or curse Him. He didn't think Job would worship and praise God if things went badly. He was basically saying that God is not worthy of praise when life gets tough. When we read the account of Job, we know what is at stake and root for him to hang in there. Job's suffering wasn't an earthly thing. God didn't intend to refine Job's character through his suffering. What occurred took place for reasons in another world.

When Martie and I were raising our kids, the only point of relief and hope we had at times was to keep saying to each other, "This too shall pass." One of the hopes we have as believers is that whatever we are going through will not last forever. The troubles will not only be resolved but will make sense. We will see that there was good and glory and gain to the kingdom through our struggle. So I think it's important that we caution ourselves and not build up false expectations for life in this world.

> *God wants us to be still and let Him manage the outcomes, not only in regard to timing but also in regard to method.*

God wants us to be still and let Him manage the outcomes, not only in regard to timing but also in regard to *method*. He's in charge of the *way* the problem is resolved. Usually we can think of a few specific things we want God to do. But we have to let go of the problem and relax in His power, presence, protection, and reputation. Let Him manage. Our job is to stay intimately and faithfully connected all the way through to the end.

I have had the privilege to work with CoMission, a group comprised of team members from Christian organizations in the United States who are active in ministry to public school teachers in the former Soviet Union. CoMission workers teach the Russian teachers courses in Christian life and ethics so that they in turn can teach this material to their students. In this former communist stronghold that once used the educational system to indoctrinate future generations of the Soviet Union with godless communism, the gospel has now been able to traffic. And heaven will be massively populated with the harvest that has come through the work of CoMission.

The strange thing is that the Ministry of Education in Russia invited us to do this. We often wondered why it was that a high-level bureaucrat in the Ministry of Education named Alexi Brudenov would have done such a thing. One day we learned the background.

In the late 1980s, just as *perestroika* was beginning and before CoMission came into being, Paul Eshleman, who leads the *Jesus* film project with Campus Crusade, was invited to show the film at a festival in Moscow. He marveled at the incredible opportunity opened to him. He signed a contract with theater owners in Russia to have the film shown all over the Soviet Union. There was an exclusivity clause in the contract that said that the film would never be shown on television while it was being shown in the theaters in order to protect the theater owners' financial integrity.

Just a few weeks after the contract was signed and sent out to the theaters, it was discovered that the liaison that had helped arrange the contract had sold rights to television producers on the side as well and thus breached the contract. Paul thought everything had been ruined. How disappointing that one of the first legal arrangements Western evangelicals ever made in the Soviet system was brought to shame as the contract was broken. But this did *not* mean that God was failing to protect the ministry of the film.

A few years after the film was introduced in Russia, at a dinner in Moscow, Alexi Brudenov stood up and said, "I've never been able to say this before, but several years ago while sitting at home I saw the last ten minutes of the *Jesus* film. I had never seen anything like that before and was struck with curiosity. Later, as I was walking down the street, I passed a theater whose marquee was advertising the *Jesus* film. I cried twice. I cried when I saw them nail Christ's hands to the cross, and I cried when I accepted Christ as my Savior at the close of the film."

This was an encounter with the sovereignty and wisdom of God, who, in the midst of all the chaos in Russia then, was working and moving so that one bureaucrat could be won to Christ, which opened the door of the whole Soviet Union to the gospel on the educational front!

Connect until you experience Him taking the chaos and bringing it to great and glorious conclusions. Connect with God's character and conduct. By faith, hang on and don't ever let go. We experience intimacy with God as we see and experience the reality of His presence in our lives and stand in awe of who He is and what He does in and through us.

RAFTING

Have you ever been white-water rafting? You probably know that the danger level of white-water rafting is rated on a scale of 1 to 6. Level 6 is life threatening. The ride I went on was rated level 2. As I got into the raft and we started down the river, I found myself wondering, *What's the big deal? This doesn't look difficult.* It was a beautiful day. There were wildflowers on the bank and beautiful trees and birds. I sat back in the raft and thought how great it was. Then I heard something . . . down around the bend.

Did you ever hear something down around the bend of life?

As we turned the corner, I could see the steam and spray rising. The closer we came, the louder the sound. I saw jagged rocks and water in random turmoil. If this was only a "2" ride, I would have hated to have been on a "3"! I grabbed the raft and looked back to see if the guide at the stern maneuvering his oar to guide us through the rapids was concerned. We dove and dipped around the rocks. I didn't breathe the whole way through. It was traumatic! But then the danger began to subside and the water leveled out again. I could lean back again and enjoy the ride.

I found it interesting that the guy in the back of the raft with the paddle wasn't traumatized at all. He had been through those rapids many times. He knew where every rock was and where every current went. He knew it all. As long as he was on my raft, I should have relaxed and enjoyed the ride the whole way through the turbulent stream.

> *But those who live connectedly can take a deep breath, relax, and know God and in the process have a firsthand intimate experience with His keeping power.*

Life's a lot like white-water rafting. We just need to know who is in the raft with us.

When we trust God we are never alone. God rides our raft. Every time. He has been through the waters many times with people just like you and me. He knows where the rocks are. He knows how to get us through. And the best part is that He will never leave our raft. The only jeopardy would be to try and maneuver the rapids on our own.

But those who live connectedly can take a deep breath, relax, and know God and in the process have a firsthand intimate experience with His keeping power. They will take the next set of rapids knowing Him better and relaxing more quickly. It's a privilege that only those who connectedly trust Him can experience.

ten

GREAT EXPECTATIONS

Getting Past the Myths about Intimacy

And I will dwell in the house of the Lord forever.
—Psalm 23:6

If you're reading this book because you are expecting intimacy to arrive as a blast of the Spirit that will cover you twenty-four hours a day for the rest of your life with an eternal season of ecstatic praise, warm feeling, and tangible chumminess with the Almighty God of the universe, then this chapter is going to be a disappointment to you. In fact, if these are the hopes and dreams of your soul in your search for intimacy with God, then my guess is that you probably won't even make it through the chapter.

Our longing for intimacy needs to feed in the pasture of biblical reality lest we look for more than God has promised. What does God tell us that we can truly expect as we search for intimacy with Him?

Expectations are everything. If we expect our spouses to be home at a certain time for dinner, and they aren't; if we expect our teenage son to come home early enough so that we can use the car to make our tee time, and he doesn't . . . it's a problem. When we expect friendship to be pleasant, rewarding, and uncomplicated, and it isn't; when we expect to receive that raise, that bonus, that promotion, and we don't; we inevitably feel disappointment, then discouragement, and finally despair if the broken expectation is big enough.

Some time ago I was chatting with a couple of our nation's leading Christian counselors. I asked them if they were to make a list of the most prevalent root problems in people's lives, what would be on it? Without pausing they both blurted, "Bitterness. It's on the top of the list." They went on to say that bitterness often is rooted in ill-defined expectations and a misplaced point of ultimate trust. If we expect life to be nice . . . if we expect people not to use, manipulate, ignore, misunderstand, or abuse us . . . if we expect something outside the span of reality, then it's inevitable that our dreams will become nightmares.

COMING HOME IS A PROCESS

Finding satisfaction, sustenance, and security in our relationship with God is a process. Too many of us have become discouraged in the pursuit of God by expecting that the product will be ours quickly and that the experience will be in line with our expectations of what it ought to be.

What can we realistically expect? As we have learned, the first task in the pursuit of intimacy is to deal with the disconnectedness that keeps us far from home. This is our responsibility. God looks for repentant, radically reliant hearts in which to set up His residence.

Finding satisfaction, sustenance, and security in our relationship with God is a process.

Having dealt with life in the far country, the next step is starting on a pilgrimage toward God by being routinely faithful to the realities that trigger an experience with His fulfilling presence. When we are faithful about the process of connecting to God, He is consistently faithful about fulfilling us in His time and in His way. Each of us will experience Him differently. And He will respond to us differently at different seasons and intervals of life. The consistency and constancy of His reality in our lives will be a lifelong growth experience.

Intimacy with God must not be defined in terms of its experiential elements. Experiences are too subjective, varied, and individualized to nail down as universal scenarios of intimacy. God doesn't meet all of us in the same way—emotionally, intellectually, or spiritually. Each of us perceives things in a unique way. If we define intimacy by what it looks and feels like, we will inevitably be defining it as one individual sees it, thus setting up other people for disappointment. When we read biographies of Christians or hear people tell of close encounters they have had with God, we shouldn't try to frame our own experiences to match theirs. God meets us where we are and not where someone else is.

While none of us experience God in precisely the same way, all of us do come home by way of the same road map. We do the process; God responds with an individualized product. In fact, this is what Scripture teaches us when we are told to "draw near to God and He will draw near to you" (James 4:8). That is a process statement.

I remember talking with a quality-control expert about his job as a consultant to some of the leading industries in America. I had always thought that quality control was about standing at the end of the line, looking products over, and, if they were not made well, sending them back to be rebuilt. Wrong! He told me that the key to quality control was to create a process that was effective and efficient. If the process was right, the product was guaranteed. It was the process that guaranteed the product.

Good processes depend on clear definitions. If our definitions are not right, the whole process will be misdirected and misunderstood. Intimacy requires a clear understanding of what it is, what it is not, and how to know if we are indeed tracking toward God.

What is the operational definition of the process that keeps our soul turned toward home? The pursuit of intimacy is *an intentional commitment to take steps toward God and, in the process of that Godward motion, to grow more deeply conscious of, connected to, and confident in Him alone as the only source to satisfy, sustain, and secure.*

The pursuit of intimacy is a process that is intentional. It is a process in that it is a lifelong adventure with increasing measures of satisfaction and meaning. It is intentional in that no one is zapped into intimacy; we must be actively focused on the pursuit.

The pursuit is a nonnegotiable commitment on our part to actively apply the principles that God has given us and to patiently and persistently build our lives around them. As we have learned, these principles include

- a repentant turnaround in attitude and action;

- a repudiation of self-sufficiency that leads to a radical reliance on Christ;
- a conscious connecting in ongoing communication; and
- a connecting with Him in creation, in His character and conduct, in worship and praise, in crisis, and in faithful obedience.

A commitment to these principles empowers my consciousness of Christ, my connectedness to Christ, and my confidence in Christ. The pursuit of intimacy with God embraces a way of life that increasingly fills my soul with the satisfaction, sustenance, and security of His presence. The pursuit of intimacy is about growing more deeply connected to Christ as the ultimate source for all that I need.

FIVE MYTHS ABOUT INTIMACY WITH CHRIST

While it's important to have a definition of the pursuit of intimacy as our starting point, we should not allow myths that distort our perspective to sabotage the process. Part of defining deals with clarifying what is not true as well as embracing what is true.

Myth # 1: Intimacy is primarily about what He will do for us when we get close.

The process of intimacy should never be motivated by what God might do for us but rather by our desire to do what we can for Him.

In 1985 the championship for the East Division of the American League came down to one game at the end of the season. Frank Tanana was on the mound for the Detroit Tigers and pitched a brilliant game to bring his team to victory, 2 to 1. I still remember seeing the picture of Frank, arms lifted in ecstatic celebration, on the cover of the next day's *USA Today* and reading all the praise of the press for what a great pitcher he was.

Several days later Frank pitched in the American League championship series. If the Tigers could clinch this championship, they would advance to the World Series. But Frank didn't do as well this time. In fact, the Tigers lost the game and ultimately the series. This time the talk was all about Frank's less-than-spectacular performance.

I was Frank's pastor, and a few days after the game I asked him, "How do you deal with being a hero one minute and the bad guy the next?" He said to me, "Joe, I learned something a long time ago about baseball fans. The deal with baseball fans is they all live by 'What have you done for me today?' That's all that counts."

Later I reflected on his comments and realized that same attitude characterizes a lot of us as God's people. When we think about intimacy it's easy to envision it in terms of, "What has God done for me *lately*?" We tend to validate His reality and measure the quality of our relationship to Him by what He is doing for us at any given moment and by the frequency and intensity of His interventions in our lives. Is there any one of us who hasn't assumed that the reality of God and the quality of our relationship to Him is measured by how many times He drops into our lives and does something good and spectacular?

When this is our expectation, we quickly grow disinterested, discouraged, and even dysfunctional in our walk with Him. In my own life I've often felt cheated. If I hear someone talk about the marvelous intervention of God in his life and how spectacular God has been for him, I begin to wonder why God never does anything like that for me.

Do you ever feel abnormal—spiritually abnormal—because God just doesn't seem to be doing a lot for you? Have you ever felt a lack of spiritual self-esteem, as though maybe you're not all that important to God? Or have you ever felt as though He might well be the God of our fathers but was surely out of the office in our generation? It's kind of like Lewis Carroll's *Alice in Wonderland*, where the complaint is lodged: "Jam tomorrow, and jam yesterday, but never jam today."

I think that's why a lot of us are seduced by anything that is spiritually experiential. If the recipe comes in the guise of Christianity, even if it's wildly exotic, we flock to it so that we can sense that God is doing something "real" for us. Rather than continuing faithfully to take the routine steps toward God in our pilgrimage, we wait by the side of the road looking for a holy handout. It's always easier to opt for the quick hit, the rush of spiritual adrenaline, than to focus on the long haul.

Rangers in Yellowstone Park tell us that in spite of all the signs that say "Don't feed the bears," people are constantly doing just that. As a result rangers have to pick up dead bears in the woods that die from starvation because tourists weren't there to feed them. If there are no handouts for two weeks, the bears die. And to think that the woods are full of nourishment! The bears could have gotten busy doing what they were built to do, but instead they died because they tried to get by on the easy handouts.

We are like those bears. God has provided an abundance of things for us to feed on if we are tracking toward Him through prayer, Bible reading, and fellowship with other Christians, and practicing the commands of Scripture. If we are faithful, none of us is going to starve. In fact, our spiritual hunger should drive us to seek out more of the good things of God. He calls us to be fed and nourished by Him at the core of our beings, yet we keep looking for easy, quick hits of His presence. It makes me wonder if heaven contains signs that say, "Don't feed the Christians!" Intimacy is not about holy handouts. It is characterized by steadfast faithfulness.

We can see this truth throughout the life of Abraham. God motivated him to leave Ur of the Chaldees with a whole list of promises (Genesis 12). Abraham obeyed God even though he had not yet received the promised son. When Sarah got too old to have a baby, she and Abraham were very confused about God's will. They even tried to fulfill His will through their own maneuverings. Yet Abraham continued to worship God and track toward intimacy with Him. God kept His promise, and Isaac was born. Later, when God told Abraham to sacrifice Isaac, Abraham was faithful to the command and was willing to obey. God again kept His promise by sparing Isaac's life. Abraham committed himself to the process of obedience, and God intervened time after time with a new and deeper level of intimacy.

It's easy to think we would all be faithful if God intervened in our lives the way He did with Abraham, but we forget that the story of Abraham covers decades. The recorded interventions of God into Abraham's life average about one in every fifteen years. Think about going fifteen years without having a Bible, with no indwelling Spirit, without spiritual friends, and not hearing from God. Yet Abraham lived a life of steadfast faithfulness to God.

When Joseph was seventeen God gave him a dream that someday he would stand in great authority and even his brothers would bow to him. But that's the last dream he had from God for many years. In the meantime, as noted earlier, his jealous brothers ganged up on him and sold him as a slave. His owner's wife tried day after day to seduce him and eventually falsely accused him of attempted rape. He was sent to jail, where he helped out a guy who promised to repay the favor but forgot about him. Yet Joseph stayed faithful to God.

God could have appeared at any time and bailed Joseph out of a problem situation, but He didn't. Instead He worked behind the scenes, silently arranging the time when Joseph would emerge humbled and refined. Joseph was ready to be wonderfully used by God, and God delivered him. Joseph's simple, steadfast faithfulness led to power in his life (Genesis 41:39–45).

Job was clueless about what God was doing in his life. I find it interesting that God never explained that the devil was actually behind Job's sufferings (Job 1:1–2:6). But after Job exemplified steadfast faithfulness, God intimately revealed Himself and helped Job resolve the conflict of his soul (38:1–40:2; 40:6–41:34).

The willingness to serve faithfully while waiting to receive God's promises is not limited to Old Testament characters. Paul knew what it meant to remain steadfast in the midst of difficult circumstances. He wrote: "We are afflicted in every way, but not crushed; perplexed, but not despairing; persecuted, but not forsaken; struck down, but not destroyed; always carrying about in the body the dying of Jesus, so that the life of Jesus also may be manifested in our body" (2 Corinthians 4: 8–10). In the same context he adds: "We look not at the things which are seen, but at the things which are not seen; for the things which are seen are temporal, but the things which are not seen are eternal" (v. 18). In essence Paul was saying that our lives should be driven by the reality of eternity to come, not by here-and-now experiences.

We may think that Christianity is about God pleasing us, but Paul makes it clear that our ambition in life should be to please *Him*. That is the essence of authentic Christianity. God rarely invades our lives with dramatic interventions. And when He does, it is not only for our benefit but to reveal His glory through us (1 Chronicles 16:9–10). While it's true that God loves to be generous with us and gives us many good things, we have to remember that when it comes to the major interventions, He manages the agenda.

> *Intimacy is about faithfulness now and fulfillment then . . . in God's time.*

Romance requires our steadfast faithfulness—as well as our charm, personality, money, and everything else—to finally win the day. But as you learn to put the other person first, you discover the joy of what love is all about. You won't know the thrill of an intimate relationship until you faithfully pursue the other person.

So it is with our relationship to God. In the pursuit of God we are responsible for routine faithfulness. Eventually the reward will come. Intimacy is about faithfulness *now* and fulfillment *then* . . . in God's time.

Myth # 2: Intimacy is about an informal buddy-buddy relationship with God.

There's no doubt that an important element of our relationship with God is built on the fact that His Word welcomes us to call Him "Abba! Father!" (Galatians 4:6). When we are close to someone, we are usually on a first-name basis. Christ tells us that we are no longer slaves but friends (John 15:15). Yet there is far more to an ongoing relationship with God than backslapping chumminess. Intimacy with God is about being struck with His grandeur and majesty. We need to stand with reverent hearts in awe at the thought of a relationship with Him.

Think of it this way. If Christ were to walk into the room while you were reading this chapter, what would you do? When Martie gets lost in a book, my only hope is to say, "When you come out of 'book world,' I have a question I want to ask you," which usually elicits a distant, audible noise that registers as an acknowledgment of my request.

But none of us would be lost in "book world" if Christ walked into the room.

Some of us might think we would get out that list of questions we always wanted to ask Him. Others of us imagine jumping up and throwing our arms around Him and thanking Him for saving us. Perhaps the more exuberant types envision giving Him a high five for all He is and all He has done.

I can assure you that if Christ walked into the room while you were reading this book, none of the above would occur. We would fall flat on our faces before Him, feeling phenomenally undone, exposed, unworthy. Thankfully, He would come near, lift us up, and tell us not to be afraid. By His grace He would welcome us into His presence that we might know the joy of His fellowship. But our relationship with Him would always be marked by a sense of awe and respect, even when we enjoyed sweet moments of close fellowship with Him.

Myth # 3: The experience of intimacy is the same for all of us.

The expectation of a universal standard for an intimate relationship with God usually falls somewhere between highly charged emotional experiences and deep, quiet personal encounters at the depth of the soul. While both are valid ways in which we can experience intimacy with God, it is dangerous to try to pour ourselves into the mold of someone else's experience.

I've always been intrigued by the temperament and personality differences among the disciples. The breadth and mix of their differences guaranteed that none of them experienced intimacy with Christ in the same way or at the same level. There was Thomas, who was highly cognitive, wanting to analyze and reason everything through to his full satisfaction. There was Peter, who was quick, verbal, and aggressive. And there was John, who was soft, warm, and mellow. Some of us will experience intimacy with Christ as a cognitive and intellectual experience, as it probably was for Thomas. Others of us will experience intimacy in the emotional side of our beings. People from different cultures and different backgrounds and with different personalities will experience Christ in a wonderful variety of ways.

What we will have in common, as we have already learned, will not be the nature of our experience of intimacy with Christ but the process through which we move toward that intimacy. If we are to encourage one another toward deeper, more meaningful experiences with God, we should not flaunt or promote our own experiences as the standard but rather help one another stay in the process.

Myth # 4: We can experience the fullness of intimacy with God in the here and now.

It is vitally important to remember that God's Word tells us that now "we see through a glass, darkly; but then face to face" (1 Corinthians 13:12 KJV). We will never know the fullness of the joy of unhindered intimacy with God on this side of heaven. Our limitations are too severe.

We are encased in bodies and have minds that are still affected by the Fall. After Eden sweat and fatigue became a way of life. The physical state of our bodies affects our minds and emotions. When we are drained of energy, we experience God's presence in far different ways than during times of strength and vitality. If I had the opportunity, I would spend large blocks of time sitting on a cliff overlooking the vast expanse of His creation, walking through the countryside, or letting my eyes plumb the depths of the starry universe above me. The problem is, those times are few and far between.

I try to carve out time in the mornings just to spend with God. But after a wonderful time of reading His Word, praying, and meditating on Him, I have to throw myself headlong into the busyness of my day. God is still there to help and encourage me, but my day with its routines and challenges clouds the specialness of those quiet moments at the beginning of my day.

Yet my work is part of my responsibility to serve Him. We all were put on Earth to do more than experience His presence in quiet corners. Now is not the stage in life to spend all our time in contemplative solitude. The world around us needs to hear about Him. Hurting people need help. Despairing neighbors need the encouragement that only God can provide through us. Our employers need a good day's work from us.

Not being able to sense deep intimacy with God all the time should motivate us to live for the day when we will see Him face to face. Soon enough, the baggage of our fallenness, the press of life's responsibilities, will be lifted from our backs, and the cares of this life will evaporate. In the twinkling of an eye, we will find ourselves in an eternity where the prime preoccupation will be to enjoy unhindered intimacy with Him. Forever.

Myth # 5: We can experience intimacy with a partially surrendered life.

The experience of true intimacy with God does not require perfection, but it does require that we be fully surrendered. Full surrender means that we live with an attitude of unlimited obedience. Though we may fail, an immediate response of repentance that refuses to let us become entrenched in our failure will keep us on the path toward home.

It would be hard to believe that we could have intimacy in an earthly relationship in the fullest, most rewarding sense if we were living in continuing offense toward the one with whom we were seeking to develop intimacy. Many marriages suffer a loss of intimacy because one of the partners has ceased to be loyal. Lying to or cheating on a spouse, ignoring the other's needs, using the relationship for your own benefit when it's convenient, and neglecting responsibilities when it's convenient are all prescriptions for a quick distancing between two hearts.

So it is with God. All through Scripture God requires that we give Him the totality of our beings. We are to love the Lord our God with all our heart, strength, and mind (see Deuteronomy 6:5; Matthew 22:37; Mark 12:30). In the letters Christ wrote to the churches in the early chapters of the book of Revelation, it was their ongoing, undealt-with sin and shortcomings that shortchanged their relationship with Christ.

We cannot expect intimacy when we live like the person who said:

I'd like to buy three dollars' worth of God.
    Please, not enough to explode my soul or disturb my sleep, but just enough to equal a cup of warm milk or a snooze in the

sunshine. I don't want enough of Him to make me love a black man or pick beets with a migrant.

I want ecstasy, not transformation. I want the warmth of the womb, not a new birth. I want about a pound of the eternal in a paper sack.

I'd like to buy about three dollars' worth of God, please.

FIVE TRUTHS ABOUT INTIMACY WITH GOD

Pushing the myths aside clears the way for the process of our progress toward God to take hold. It opens a realistic door to knowing and experiencing Him at new and rewarding levels.

I think I have a major starch deficiency in my life because I'm passionately addicted to things like potatoes, rice, and pasta. I can't get enough of them. If Martie is away for an evening, when she returns she will inevitably ask me what I had for supper while she was gone. I have to tell her I just boiled some pasta and put a little butter and salt and pepper on it. She just looks at me in amazement.

What is more amazing to me is that often, when I'm full of pasta, I still want more.

That's like the wonder and joy of growing toward intimacy—we can never get enough of Christ. It's a never-ending, increasingly rewarding process. To help encourage the process, here are five truths that replace the distracting myths about intimacy with God.

These truths help us form realistic expectations about intimacy.

Truth #1: Our primary purpose in life is to embrace the transcendent God by faith and to worship Him in purity and service.

This life-focus is a directional thing. Intimacy is not about God doing things for me. It's not about Him making me feel good. It's about this: I embrace the transcendent God of the universe and pledge to worship and serve Him no matter what happens. When the arrows of my passions and worship point from me to Him, I've successfully reversed the direction of my expectations. And as I worship Him with the purity of my life and the service of my hands, I can say with Job, no matter what happens, "Though He slay me, I will hope in Him" (13:15). Intimacy begins by giving self away. It gives self to God as the ultimate gift of our love.

Truth #2: God intervenes in dramatic ways only periodically and selectively for major purposes in His kingdom and the blessings of His people.

That ought to be enough for us. It should be sufficient to hear about or to see God's work in somebody else's life and say, "Isn't that just like my God? I love to see God busy!" Instead we tend to feel sorry for ourselves and complain, "That never happens to me. Why isn't God busy about me?" We should learn to rest and rejoice in the fact that God does marvelous things in others' lives, and that if our need ever gets dramatic enough or our place in His plan ever gets strategic enough, He'll do something dramatic for us as well. Until then, we need to be forever grateful for His daily presence; His quiet work behind the scenes; His grace that is sufficient; His mercy that stays His judgment; and heaven.

Truth #3: God has already done more for me than I deserve.

If God never does anything more than redeem us cancel hell and guarantee heaven if He never does anything more than that, He has already done more than we deserve. That ought to be enough to launch me in praise and worship for the rest of my life.

Think about it. God has already dramatically intervened in a major way in our lives when He opened up the story of the cross to us and bid us come by the power of His Spirit. When we embraced that rugged cross and felt the weight of our sin leave us and were washed by His cleansing blood, it was enough. More than enough to keep our hearts lovingly grateful.

Truth #4: God is probably doing a lot of things for us that we do not even know about.

These may not be big, dramatic things, but God's Word teaches us that He stands like a sovereign sentinel at the gates of our lives, keeping out anything that is more than we can bear (1 Corinthians 10:13). He only lets in those things that He, by His power and with our cooperation, will turn to His glory and gain and to our good. Paul declares in Romans 8:28, "We know that God causes all things to work together for good to those who love God, to those who are called according to His purpose."

Why then do we put our head on the pillow at night and murmur, "Where were You today, God? You didn't answer my prayer. Nothing big happened. The day was flat and dull." Instead, we should say with hearts full of gratitude, "Lord, thanks for being busy in my life today in stuff I don't even know about. You, by the power of Your angels, have protected me from the enemy who sought to destroy me. And thanks for the assurance that, as the sovereign sentinel at the gate of my life, what You did let in today, You promised that by Your power You could turn to glory and gain and good."

We have to remember that God is a lot busier in our lives than we think. For us to go around thinking that He doesn't do much for us contradicts the reality of His marvelous grace that is in our lives twenty-four hours a day: guarding, keeping, excluding, insulating, protecting, and blessing.

Truth #5: When God thinks of intimacy, He thinks of a heart relationship with us.

We're like kids at Christmas begging, "Give me the gift! Give me the gift!" and forgetting that it's out of love that the gifts were given to us by our parents. Of course our parents love to give and bless us with gifts, but what they really want is a love relationship with us. Intimacy is about a relationship, not a gift exchange. When we live expectantly, serve Him purely, slow down and spend seasons on our knees with His Word in prayer and meditation, He fills our souls with Himself.

God doesn't meet us at the mall. He seeks us in the inner sanctum of our hearts. If it's intimacy we want, we need to be more intrigued with the Giver than the gifts. It's not the stuff He does for us that we should be loving; it's *Him*. If we want to

> *When we live expectantly, serve Him purely, slow down and spend seasons on our knees with His Word in prayer and meditation, He fills our souls with Himself.*

experience Him more than we do, we need to love Him more than we do—more than all those other things we are attracted to, more than all the provisions we expect from Him.

GREAT EXPECTATIONS

From the Old Testament to the New, Scripture is about God's personal, prioritized agenda for restored fellowship and a rewarding relationship that satisfies the longings of our souls and glorifies Him.

A successful pilgrimage toward intimacy not only demands that we replace faulty or unbalanced expectations with truthful ones, but that we ask ourselves, *What can we expect?*

We can expect that God has promised to provide in a relationship with Him. Scripture suggests at least three attainable outcomes of a deepening personal relationship with Him: (1) He will satisfy our souls; (2) He will sustain our lives; and (3) He will secure us even in the face of great danger.

These outcomes have been mentioned frequently throughout this book, but nowhere are they more clearly defined and demonstrated than in the familiar Shepherd Psalm of David, Psalm 23. Let's examine that psalm, thinking about how we can attain these outcomes in our experiences of intimacy with God. First, let's read the psalm slowly to absorb the message and the meaning.

The LORD is my shepherd,
I shall not want.
He makes me lie down in green pastures;

He leads me beside quiet waters.
He restores my soul;
He guides me in the paths of righteousness
For His name's sake.
Even though I walk through the valley of the shadow of death,
I fear no evil, for You are with me;
Your rod and Your staff, they comfort me.
You prepare a table before me in the presence of my enemies;
You have anointed my head with oil;
My cup overflows.
Surely goodness and lovingkindness will follow me all the days of
*   my life,*
And I will dwell in the house of the LORD *forever.*

Note the dynamics of the relationship. It's not between equals; it's between a shepherd and His sheep. Sheep are radically reliant on the shepherd. Little Bo Peep's consultant was wrong: Sheep don't find their way home if you leave them alone! They require a shepherd to provide leadership, provision, and protection. The shepherd consistently tends the sheep sometimes at great sacrifice to himself.

What does the shepherd provide?

The shepherd is a source of *satisfaction* for the sheep. We need to forget about our lists of want-to's and hope-so's and dwell on what we really need. The true test of satisfaction is to be able to say with the psalmist, "I shall not want." Contentment doesn't mean that we won't have a desire for additional commodities or better relationships. It means that those desires don't drive and manage our lives. It means that we allow God to be the provider while we are content with Him. The psalmist paints this picture of satisfaction: "He makes me lie down in green pastures; He leads me beside quiet waters. He restores my soul." Note the satisfying components of provision, peace, and recovery.

If you've ever walked the hills of England or spent time where sheep are part of the agrarian economy, you know that there are few pictures of contentment clearer than the psalmist's picture of sheep who, though they sometimes wander, never intentionally run away but find themselves fully satisfied in the care and provision of their shepherd.

To be content is to be satisfied with God.

The picture of God's *securing* work is reflected in the psalmist's response to facing his enemies in the valley of the shadow of death. He testifies that God has made him so secure that he can dine in the presence of his enemies and fearlessly walk through the valley of death if that were necessary. Why? Because God is with him. The reality of His rod (protecting work) and His staff (rescuing and guiding work) secure the psalmist.

The presence of God brings with it all that God is. He doesn't leave pieces and parts of Himself behind. He blesses us with the fullness of His partnership in our lives. His presence guarantees His protecting power, His sovereign direction, His unsurpassed wisdom, His tender loving care, and His just involvement in our lives. To be afraid, to permit fear to shadow our souls, is to deny His presence. Yet embracing by faith the reality of His presence convinces us that He will fully secure us. Regardless.

The final verses conclude with God's *sustaining* work. The psalmist's peace while dining in front of his enemies reflects the pleasure of being sustained by Him. He speaks of God's sustaining work in his life as an overflowing cup, and then he

> *Satisfaction with God is beginning to take hold when we cease being driven and defined by earthly things and begin to long for spiritual realities.*

marvels that the goodness and lovingkindness of God will follow him every day of his life. The psalmist celebrates ultimate sustenance as he anticipates that someday he will dwell in the house of the Lord forever.

We know that intimacy is working when we can say with David, "The LORD is my shepherd, I shall not want." When we can honestly say that we really don't need additional things to be satisfied, sustained, and secured, then we will know that we are a long way down the road toward coming home, toward connecting intimately with the God who offers all of Himself to us.

Satisfaction with God is beginning to take hold when we cease being driven and defined by earthly things and begin to long for spiritual realities. Paul affirms this dynamic in his own testimony in Philippians 4:10–13.

> But I rejoiced in the Lord greatly, that now at last you have revived your concern for me; indeed, you were concerned before, but you lacked opportunity. Not that I speak from want, for I have learned to be content in whatever circumstances I am. I know how to get along with humble means, and I also know how to live in prosperity; in any and every circumstance I have learned the secret of being filled and going hungry, both of having abundance and suffering need. I can do all things through Him who strengthens me.

When we find our all in Him, our lives will be marked by an unshakable confidence that lies beneath the surface tremors of our daily activities. This is the confidence that only comes when we are connected to the fact that He will be all that He says He is; that He will be there for us, whether we feel it or not; and that He cannot deny either His character or His promises. This sense of intimate sustenance comes to those who by faith connect to a God who will never leave them or forsake them.

This security that comes with intimacy with God is marked by an undaunted sense of courage. We will say with Paul,

> Who will separate us from the love of Christ? Will tribulation, or distress, or persecution, or famine, or nakedness, or peril, or sword? Just as it is written, "For Your sake we are being put to death all day long; we were considered as sheep to be slaughtered." But in all these things we overwhelmingly conquer through Him who loved us. For I am convinced that neither death, nor life, nor angels, nor principalities, nor things present, nor things to come, nor powers, nor height, nor depth, nor any other created thing, will be able to separate us from the love of God, which is in Christ Jesus our Lord (Romans 8:35–39).

NOTES

Chapter 2. Aloneness

1. J. Krishnamurti, *On Love and Loneliness* (New York: Harper San Francisco, 1993), 55.

Chapter 3. Intimacy in Perspective

1. "Ali, Muhammad," Microsoft® Encarta® 96 Encyclopedia. 1993–1995 Microsoft Corporation. All rights reserved. Funk & Wagnalls Corporation. All rights reserved.

2. David Whitman, "Was It Good for Us?" *U.S. News and World Report,* 19 May 1997, 58.

3. William Shakespeare, *Henry VIII,* 3.2.351–85.

Chapter 4. It Happened in Eden

1. Peter Kreeft, *Three Philosophies of Life* (San Francisco: Ignatius, 1989), 28.

Chapter 5. Drifting Away from God

1. Peter Kreeft, *Three Philosophies of Life* (San Francisco: Ignatius, 1989), 22.

2. Elisabeth Elliot, *Shadow of the Almighty* (New York: Harper, 1958), 50.

3. "Jones Books His Place in US Open Legend," *The Times,* 18 June 1996, 50.

4. Ibid.

5. Steve Farrar, *Finishing Strong: Finding the Power to Go the Distance* (Sisters, Ore.: Questar, Multnomah Books, 1995), 29.

Chapter 6. Who's That Knocking?

1. Thomas Keating, *Intimacy with God* (New York: Crossroad, 1994), 22.

2. Laurence Shames, *The Hunger for More* (New York: Time Books, 1989), preface, x.

3. Ibid., 80.

Chapter 7. Repentant Reliance

1. F. Laubach, "Conversion, Penitence, Repentance, Proselyte," in the *New International Dictionary of New Testament Theology,* ed. Colin Brown, vol. 1, rev. ed. (Grand Rapids: Zondervan, 1986), 353.

2. Nigel Turner, *Syntax,* vol. 3 of *Grammar of New Testament Greek,* ed. J. H. Moulton et al. (Edinburgh: T&T Clark, 1963), 75.

3. H. C. Leupold, *Exposition of Genesis,* vol. 1 (Grand Rapids: Baker, 1942), 227.

4. C. F. Keil and F. Delitzsch, *The Pentateuch,* vol. 1 of *Biblical Commentary on the Old Testament* (1875; reprint, Grand Rapids: Eerdmans, 1968), 119.

5. Robert Baker Girdlestone, *Synonyms of the Old Testament* (1897; reprint, Grand Rapids: Eerdmans, 1948), 38.

6. J. R. MacDuff, *Morning and Night Watches* (London: James Nisbet, 1852), 80–82.

Chapter 8. Connectedness

1. Ravi Zacharias, *Christian Daily Planner* (Dallas: Word, 1977), a publication prepared by Ravi Zacharias International Ministries.

2. Bill Bright, founder of Campus Crusade for Christ, died in 2003. I had the opportunity to speak with him about his personal Bible study and prayer life several years before his death.

NOTE TO THE READER

The publisher invites you to share your response to the message of this book by writing Discovery House Publishers, Box 3566, Grand Rapids, MI 49501, USA. For information about other Discovery House books, music, or videos, contact us at the same address or call 1-800-653-8333. Find us on the Internet at http://www.dhp.org/ or send e-mail to books@dhp.org.

ABOUT THE AUTHOR

Joe Stowell serves as Teaching Pastor at Harvest Bible Chapel. Before coming to Harvest, he served as the seventh president of Moody Bible Institute. His first love is Jesus Christ and preaching His Word. An internationally recognized conference speaker, Joe has written numerous books including the daily devotional *Strength for the Journey, The Upside of Down, Eternity*, and his latest release, *From the Front Lines*. In addition to his service at Harvest, Dr. Stowell is a Ministry Partner with RBC Ministries in Grand Rapids, Michigan, partnering in media production. He also serves on the Board of the Billy Graham Evangelistic Association. Joe and his wife Martie are the parents of three adult children and ten grandchildren. They make thier home in suburban Chicago.